Theory of Customs Unions

Theory of Customs Unions

AM EL-AGRAA & AJ JONES

St Martin's Press New York

 For information, write:
St. Martin's Press, Inc., 175 Fifth Avenue, New York, NY 10010
Printed in Great Britain
First published in the United States of America in 1981

ISBN 0–312–79737–0

Library of Congress Cataloging in Publication Data

El-Agraa, A M
Theory of customs unions.

Bibliography: p.
Includes indexes.
1. Customs unions. I. Jones, A. J., joint author. II. Title.
HF1713.E54 1981 382.91'01 80–23422
ISBN 0–312–79737–0

To our families

Contents

Preface

Our aim in writing this book is to dispel the notion that the theory of customs unions has become sterile. The book is written for those with a general interest in international economics and particularly for those interested in international economic integration. It deals with the theory of customs unions rather than with international economic integration in general, since it contains no discussion of the problems of common markets and similar associations – these are tackled in A.M. El-Agraa (ed.) *The Economics of the European Community* (Philip Allan and St. Martin's Press 1980).

We should like to thank our students for persevering with us while the contents of this book were being tested on them. We should also like to thank the clerical staff of the School of Economic Studies at the University of Leeds for all their typing assistance.

A M EL-AGRAA
A J JONES

August 1980

1

Introduction

Types of Economic Integration

The field of international economics called international economic integration is concerned with the discriminatory removal of all trade impediments between participating nations and with the establishment of certain elements of co-operation and co-ordination between them. The latter depends entirely on the form that integration takes. Different types of integration can be envisaged:

(a) *sectoral integration*, i.e. the removal of barriers to trade in the output of a single industrial sector as, for example, in the European Coal and Steel Community (ECSC);
(b) *free trade areas* where member countries abolish all trade impediments among themselves but retain their freedom with regard to the determination of their policies *vis-à-vis* the outside world (non-participants), e.g. the European Free Trade Association (EFTA), which excludes agricultural products from its arrangements; the Latin American Free Trade Area (LAFTA), etc;
(c) *customs unions*, which are very much like free trade areas, except that member countries are obliged to conduct common external relations. For instance, they must adopt common external tariffs on imports from the outside world – the European Economic Community

(EEC) is, in this sense, a customs union, but there is more to it than just that;

(d) *common markets*, which are customs unions that also allow for free factor mobility across national member boundaries, i.e. capital, labour and enterprise should move without hindrance between the participating nations, e.g. the East African Common Market (EACM), the EEC (which is a common market, but again there is more to it), etc;

(e) *complete economic unions*, which are common markets that call for complete unification of monetary and fiscal policies, i.e. there is a central authority which controls these aspects so that existing nations become regions of the union;

(f) *complete political integration* where the participants become literally one nation, i.e. the central authority not only controls monetary and fiscal policies but also has a central parliament with the sovereignty of a nation's government.

Since the end of the Second World War, many schemes for international economic integration have been proposed and a number have been implemented, though undoubtedly the major stimulus to academic interest has been provided by the development of the EEC. Although many of the originators of this scheme regarded it as merely a step along the road towards a more complete form of economic and political integration, the major detailed provisions of the Treaty of Rome 1957, by which the EEC was created, relate simply to the formation of a customs union. It is thus not surprising that analytical interest should also focus mainly on the problems of customs union formation and abstract from the more far-reaching issues of economic integration by the (often implicit) assumptions (a) that there is no international mobility of factor services and (b) that domestic economic policies remain as being independently chosen in pursuit of purely national objectives. Although analytical interest in the subject of economic integration has broadened, particularly in response to proposals for further economic and monetary integration in the EEC, it remains the case that the most thoroughly developed framework of thought in this field still relates to the particular issues of customs union formation. It is this on which we concentrate here and readers interested in the wider issues relating to the EEC are referred to El-Agraa (1980), whilst Balassa (1976) and Machlup (1977) provide, respectively, a brief outline of the most important integration schemes and a comprehensive listing of historical writings on integration projects.

The Theory of Customs Unions

The theory of customs unions is a relatively recent branch of economic analysis. Although Machlup has traced the history of thought on the subject further back, he agrees (Machlup 1977, p.258) that it is Viner's pioneering distinction between trade creation and trade diversion (Viner 1950) which can be credited with opening up this new branch of the theory of commercial policy. For Viner, trade creation occurs when the formation of a customs union leads to the replacement of high cost production in one partner by imports from a lower cost producer in another member of the union. Trade diversion, on the other hand, results when (tariff-free) imports from a partner replace lower cost imports from the rest of the world which are excluded by the discriminatory effect of the common external tariff. Unfortunately, the apparent simplicity of these concepts is misleading. Viner failed to provide a complete theoretical framework for his analysis and much of the subsequent literature on the subject illustrates the confusion that has arisen from the initial vagueness.

One strand of analysis has employed a partial equilibrium approach (see, for example, Meade 1955a, Humphrey and Ferguson 1960, Johnson 1962 & 1965a, Cooper and Massell 1965a, and Corden 1972) and is notable for the relative simplicity with which many important results have first been introduced into the literature. A second and now the dominant strand of analysis is provided by the general equilibrium approach derived from the orthodox theory of trade policy. This seems to have been first applied to customs union theory by Lipsey in his doctoral dissertation but, as this was not published as a book until much later (Lipsey 1970), it was his well-known survey article (Lipsey 1960) which did most to initiate the development of this approach, which forms the basis, for example, of two notable books on the subject (Vanek 1965 and Kemp 1969), as well as for the second important survey article on developments in customs union theory (Krauss 1972).

This three-country, two-commodity, two-factor general equilibrium approach lends itself to geometrical exposition but, unfortunately, the literature has relied entirely on the tools of commodity space, such as production and consumption possibility frontiers and offer curves, rather than on what we regard as the simpler techniques of general equilibrium demand and supply analysis. Accordingly, one objective in writing this book is to show how these techniques can be related both to the underlying assumptions of the model and to the partial equilibrium approach. This is done in Chapter 2, in which the main variants of the basic model of a small open economy are also examined in the context of the traditional approach to customs union analysis in an attempt to eliminate the terminological confusion which continues to surround the different effects associated with customs union formation.

A second objective, pursued in Chapter 3, is to investigate the differences between free trade areas and customs unions. It is unfortunately true that traditional customs union theory has largely overlooked the distinction between these two forms of regional economic integration because it has concentrated on the one step which is common to both, i.e. the removal of all impediments to trade between members. As subsequent chapters attempt to show, however, an integral part of customs union analysis should concern the choice and adoption of the common external tariff. Such a step is not involved in the formation of a free trade area and it therefore seems appropriate to enquire what differences flow from the fact that members of free trade areas can maintain independent trade policies *vis-à-vis* the rest of the world, whilst relying on 'rules of origin' to prevent the phenomenon known as 'trade deflection'.

Chapters 2 and 3, however, represent attempts to tackle objectives essentially subsidiary to those which prompted us to write this book. As we see it, there are two important weaknesses in the existing literature on customs union theory. The first of these weaknesses is that, although the approach to the general theory of trade policy has been radically transformed in recent years, this transformation has not yet permeated many contributions to customs union theory. Corden has characterised this transformation as being the third stage in the development of the theory of trade policy (Corden 1974, Chapter 1). All three stages employ the same basic theoretical framework – as set out in Chapter 2 below – but differ in their treatment of government policy within the framework.

In the first stage only a simplified version of the basic framework is considered, with assumptions chosen to produce the result that the free working of the economy without government intervention of any kind will produce an efficient allocation of resources and satisfy the Paretian conditions for welfare maximisation. Within such a framework, which may also be identified as the traditional ('small country') framework of customs union theory employed, for example, by Lipsey (1960), Michaely (1965 and 1976), and Bhagwati (1971), any government intervention (other than by lump sum transfers to redistribute wealth) will produce a distortion from these Paretian conditions and hence result in a reduction in the level of economic welfare. This is just as true of taxes on production, employment or consumption as of taxes on trade. In each case government action is seen as reducing welfare and, if taken at face value, the theoretical framework provides a simple rationale for the policy of free trade as a special case of *laissez-faire*.

In the second stage of the development of the theory of trade policy, it was recognised that, if the simplified version of the basic framework was modified in various ways that could be interpreted as increasing the realism of the model, then, with no other government action being contemplated in the model, at least some taxes on trade could be shown to be superior to a policy of free trade. This stage thus appeared to provide a variety of arguments for protection. In the context of customs union theory, such modifications to the traditional model are exemplified by Yu and Scully (1976) and Floystad

(1975) and, as with the second stage of the development of general trade policy theory, the main method of analysis is to compare the results of various arbitrarily chosen forms of trade policy.

The third stage in the development of thought was foreshadowed by the development of the theory of optimum tariffs (see, for example, Graaff 1949–50) and owes much to the pioneering work of Meade (1955b). Its effective popularisation, however, came with the development of optimal intervention analysis, which can be mainly attributed to the work of Johnson (in particular see Johnson 1965b). As in the second stage of thought, various kinds of distortions from the Paretian conditions for welfare maximisation are recognised, as is the possible existence of certain non-economic objectives of government policy but, in this third stage, other forms of government intervention are also contemplated, in addition to the use of trade policy. For any given distortion or non-economic objective the outcome of alternative policies can then be compared and ranked so that, with the assumption that governments seek to use the best available policy, this theoretical approach can be viewed either as a guide to rational policy decisions or as a means of explaining and predicting actual policy choices. In Corden's view this transformation of the theory of trade policy does much to restore the case for free trade, although a few valid uses for trade taxes can be identified (1974, especially Chapter 1, part 1 and Chapter 15). It has to be realised, however, that the recognition of socio-political constraints on the use of certain policy instruments allows various 'second-best' explanations to be given for the actual use of trade policy.

Corden's book provides an admirable account of the application of this modern approach to the general theory of trade policy, but deliberately excludes the consideration of all forms of policy changes which discriminate according to the country of origin of the trade, and few contributions to customs union theory seem to have been influenced by this approach. An influential early exception to this was provided by one of Johnson's many formidable contributions to the theory of tariffs (Johnson 1965a) and another exception of note is the formal statement of some of the propositions of customs union theory by Takayama (1972, Chapter 16), following the obscure but important paper of Negishi (1969). Nonetheless, many contributions to customs union theory during the last decade including, for example, Bhagwati (1971), Floystad (1975), Michaely (1976), Yu and Scully (1976), and most recently Collier (1979), have continued to ignore this approach. Accordingly, one of our main objectives here is to provide (in Chapters 4 and 5) a statement of orthodox customs union theory set entirely in the context of this modern approach to trade policy.

Our second major objective, pursued in Chapters 6–8, is to stimulate interest in the development of an alternative theoretical framework to the orthodox approach. As already noted, second major weakness in the literature. As one of the major theoretical approaches to modelling an economy, this long-run 'price theoretic' framework has long been the subject analysis of customs union formation. We regard this as the second major weakness in the literature. As one of the major theoretical approaches to modelling an economy, this long-run 'price theoretic' framework has long been the subject of extensive criticism and, in many areas of economics, this criticism has stimulated the emergence of an alternative theoretical framework which stresses the quantity variables (especially income and employment) and the role of money, uncertainty and expectations, in determining the outcome of changes in economic policy. Although such a macroeconomic framework is widely employed in, for example, international monetary economics, it has been largely ignored in both the general theory of trade policy and in customs union theory despite, in the latter case, the pioneering efforts of A.J. Brown (Brown 1961). Of course, such a framework is itself subject to many limitations but, in our view, failing the emergence of a more satisfactory general framework, it would be useful if the issues of customs union formation were approached via at least two different basic and widely recognised frameworks, rather than relying, as at present, so exclusively on only one.

2

The Traditional Framework of Customs Union Theory

A J JONES

The General Equilibrium Model of a Small Open Economy

The orthodox framework for the theory of customs unions is provided by the standard theory of tariffs extended to recognise two separate foreign economies, 'the partner' and 'the rest of the world' as well as 'the home country'. Each of these three economies is represented by a similar general equilibrium model and, in this section, the basic outline of such a model is presented for the home economy, for the case in which it can be regarded as 'small', i.e. unable to influence significant economic variables in the foreign economies.

A crucial simplification of the model is to assume that the many commodities which are produced, consumed and traded in the modern world can be reduced for analytical purposes to two 'composite commodities'. The theoretical justification for this is provided by the composite commodity theorem discovered independently by Hicks and Leontief (Hicks 1939 and Leontief 1936). This theorem shows that such aggregation is valid, provided that the relative prices of goods included in each composite commodity are unaffected by the changes being analysed. This suggests two alternative interpretations for the two-commodity level of aggregation encountered in customs union theory. The first, which characterises the orthodox general equilibrium approach, is to regard both composite commodities as being such broad aggregates as agricultural products and manufactures or the 'importables' and 'exportables' of the home country. This interpretation is thus implicitly based on the judgement that the significant consequences of customs union formation flow from the change which this brings about in the relative price of these aggregates, whilst changes in the relative prices of goods within each aggregate are regarded as insignificant. Collier has recently challenged this judgement (Collier 1979), and it must be accepted that the desirability of developing a more disaggregated model is clear. Collier's alternative framework, however, is entirely unconvincing as the basis for a general model and exemplifies the difficulties which Lipsey and others have also encountered in trying to go beyond the two-commodity framework (see, for example, Lipsey 1970). We shall, therefore, retain this level of aggregation throughout the examination of the orthodox model.

The alternative interpretation of the two-commodity framework has been implicitly offered by the partial equilibrium approach to customs union theory. As Arrow and Hahn have pointed out, partial equilibrium analysis can be regarded as 'a special case of general equilibrium analysis' (Arrow and Hahn 1971, p. 6). It is the case where one of the two commodities identified in the model is viewed as either a single homogeneous product or else the composite formed by the relatively small range of closely-related goods produced by a single industrial sector. The second commodity is then defined as the aggregate, 'all other goods'. In general, the rationale for this level of aggregation is that the single sector being examined is so small in relation to the rest of the economy that changes affecting that sector will not have significant repercussions on relative price levels in the rest of the economy. As a number of critics of the partial equilibrium approach to customs union theory have pointed out, however, such an interpretation cannot be justified when the customs union arrangements do affect all traded goods and not simply a single 'small' sector of the economy. Clearly, it is inconsistent to view the consequences of customs union formation as the outcome of successive applications of the partial equilibrium approach to a series of small sectors. Indeed, such a partial equilibrium approach seems appropriate for the problems of economic integration only when the issues are, in fact, confined to sectoral integration.

The rejection of the partial equilibrium interpretation of the two-commodity framework, however, is often confused with rejection of the simple demand and supply curve tools of analysis, and in particular with rejection of the welfare measures associated with these. But such tools of analysis do not depend on adopting the partial equilibrium interpretation of the two-commodity approach and can be rigorously employed, given the alternative general equilibrium interpretation without significant alteration in the framework of assumptions that this employs.

Such a model of a single economy is now a standard feature of most intermediate-level textbooks in microeconomics and is perhaps set out most thoroughly in Johnson and Krauss (1974). Accordingly, only a brief outline will be provided here.

With the aggregation of factor services also being justified along the same lines as the aggregation of commodities, the 'two by two' model lends itself to geometrical exposition, the first component of which is usually the Edgeworth–Bowley box diagram, as drawn in figure 2.1. The dimensions of this box represent the important simplifying assumption that there

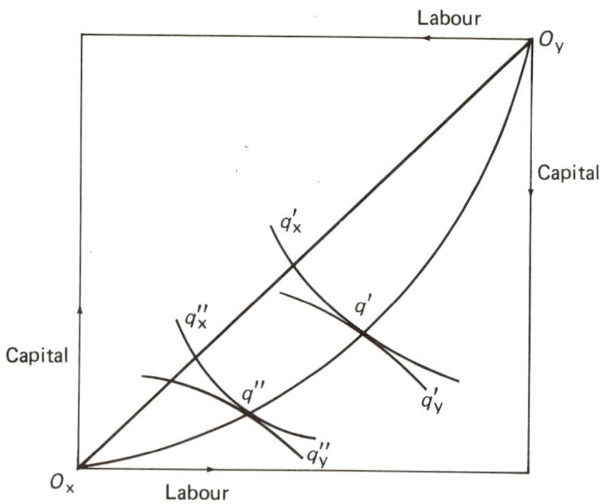

Figure 2.1 *The Edgeworth–Bowley Box Diagram of the Factor Market*

are fixed supplies of the two factor inputs within each economy. This implies that there is no international movement of factor inputs and so excludes a number of significant problems which are associated with regional economic integration schemes, notably those concerned with the rôle of multi-national companies and with the establishment of a common market for both factors and commodities, rather than simply, as here, a customs union affecting only the movement of commodities. Together with the assumption of given, perfectly known, and universally applied technology, this assumption also excludes the issues associated with economic growth (or decline) in order to focus attention on the (static) resource reallocation effects. Using O_x and O_y as the respective origins for the production functions for importables (x) and exportables (y) then allows the assumptions about technology to be displayed by the sets of isoquants, $q_x, q_x' \ldots, q_y, q_y'$, which are drawn to be consistent with the assumption of the 'law' of diminishing marginal rate of technical substitution. The points of tangency of the two sets of isoquants trace out the contract curve, $O_x q'' q' O_y$. This identifies the set of efficient allocations of the two inputs, i.e. all points on the contract curve share the characteristic that it is impossible to re-organise the use of factor inputs so as to increase output of one commodity without reducing output of the other.

Mapping this information into commodity space provides the production possibility frontier. This is drawn in figure 2.2 as $Hh''h'H_x$ to be consistent with the most widely employed variant of the set of differing assumptions that can be made about the nature of the production functions. This is that there are constant returns to scale in both industries which differ in the factor intensity of their production processes, such that, at all possible factor price levels, one of the industries (x in the case illustrated) can be identified as more labour-intensive than the other.

Although this provides us with the standard case, two alternatives are available within the same basic framework. If factor intensities are assumed to be identical in both industries, the contract curve will become the diagonal $O_x O_y$ in figure 2.1 and, when this is combined with the assumption of

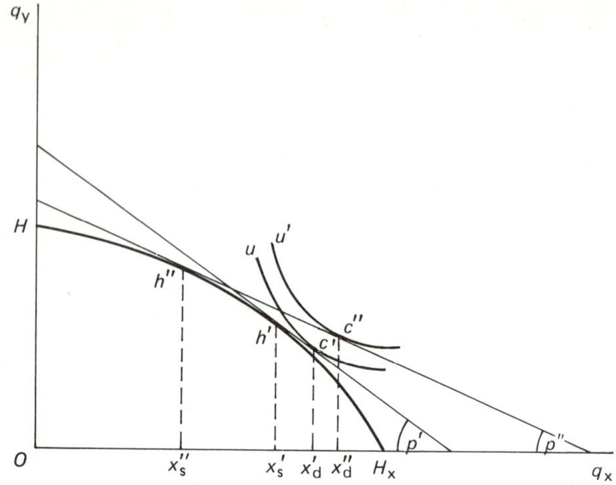

Figure 2.2 *The Commodity Market in the Two-Commodity General Equilibrium Model*

constant returns to scale, the production possibility frontier is linear. Alternatively, if increasing returns to scale are postulated, the production possibility frontier will be shown as convex to the origin.

In any of these three cases, the assumption of perfectly competitive conditions in the factor market (including perfect and costless mobility of factors between industries, factor price flexibility, and the absence of externalities associated either with employment in or production of either industry) ensures that production will occur at a point along the contract curve in factor space and along the production possibility frontier in commodity space. It is also possible in each of the three cases to transfer the information provided by the production possibility frontier to the diagrams with the axes employed in figure 2.3. This is because the variables examined in figure 2.2 are measured in terms of one of three basic units. These units are the quantities of the two commodities (q_x and q_y respectively) and the dimensions of the only price variable which is of any analytical significance. This is the relative price (terms of trade) of the two commodities and is measured in quantity units of one commodity per unit of the second. As long as it is used consistently, either commodity may serve as *numéraire* and we have here chosen to express

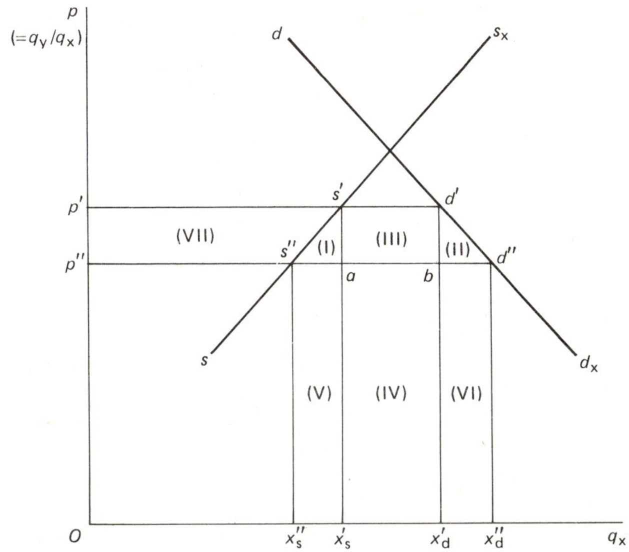

Figure 2.3 *Domestic Demand and Supply Conditions in the Home Country*

the terms of trade (p) as the relative price of the home country importables, commodity x, measured in units of commodity y per unit of x, i.e. $p = q_y/q_x$.

In figure 2.2, information in terms of this price variable is provided only by the slopes of the lines and functions drawn in the diagram. In figure 2.3, on the other hand, the price variable is clearly displayed in the vertical axis whilst the variable it replaces, q_y, is shown by the measurement of appropriate areas ($q_x \times q_y/q_x$) in that diagram. Thus the transfer of the information contained in the production possibility frontier to figure 2.3 is achieved by plotting (the absolute value of) the slope of this frontier in figure 2.2. This slope is defined as the marginal (opportunity) cost of production of commodity x and the resulting curve in figure 2.3 is hence the marginal cost curve of commodity x, ss_x. This has been drawn to correspond to the standard version of the two-commodity model displayed in figures 2.1 and 2.2 and illustrates why this is identified as the case of increasing costs. Equally, however, the two alternative versions can also be translated to diagrams like figure 2.3 and would result in (a) a horizontal marginal cost curve (i.e. the case of constant costs), or (b) a negatively inclined marginal cost curve (the case of decreasing costs).

In the standard version of increasing costs and also in the constant costs case, the further assumption of perfectly competitive conditions in the commodity market then allows us to interpret the inverse of the marginal cost function (which is, of course, also represented graphically in figure 2.3, for example, by ss_x) as the domestic supply function for commodity x. It is, I hope, obvious that this then enables us to read off from such a diagram how changes in the domestic terms of trade, e.g. from p' to p'', result in changes in the supply of commodity x. Equally, however, the fact that ss_x also represents the marginal opportunity cost curve for commodity x means that this same price change can be seen to be associated with the increase in output of y measured by $x_s''s''s'x_s'$, i.e. area (I + V). Further, the net effect of these changes on the value of national output can be measured. Thus, in figure 2.3 the y-value of the production of commodity x can be measured as $op's'x_s'$ at the terms of trade p' and as $op''s''x_s''$ at p''. Combining this change in the y-value of the production of x with the actual change in the production of y shows that the y-value of domestic production has decreased as a result of the change in the terms of trade. This fall is measured by $p's's''p''$, i.e. area (VIII), and is frequently identified as the loss in producers' surplus.[1]

It can also be noted that, if producers had not responded to the change in the terms of trade by changing the volumes of x and y produced, the effect of the change from p' to p'' would have been to decrease the y-value of the original volume of x-production by $p's'ap''$, i.e. area (VII + I), whilst production of y remained unchanged. This loss is greater than the actual loss in the y-value of producers' surplus by the amount measured by $s'as''$ i.e. area (I). This area thus shows the beneficial effect of the response of producers to the change in the relative price of the two commodities and, unlike the actual change in producers' surplus itself, is unambiguously seen as a source of gain, whether it is measured in units of x or y.

It can be emphasised that identical conclusions would flow

from the examination of the production possibility frontier and that, just as there is a one-to-one correspondence between points on the contract curve in factor space and points on the production possibility frontier in commodity space, there is also a one-to-one correspondence between points on the marginal cost curve and points on the production possibility frontier. Each of the diagrams is best suited for the display of different kinds of information, but they are all simply different ways of presenting the same basic framework and, in our view, it is the dimensions of figure 2.3 which provide the most convenient tools of analysis for the examination of the issues of customs union formation.

It must be admitted, however, that the interpretation of dd_x in that diagram as the (general equilibrium) domestic demand curve for commodity x does raise more controversial issues. It is a standard assumption that all consumers are regarded as utility-maximisers with given preferences who base their consumption plans on the income derived solely from domestic production and on the exchange possibilities which they are powerless to affect in the commodity market. To simplify the analysis it is also assumed that no tariff revenue is spent on imports. From the viewpoint of positive analysis, it can be noticed that these assumptions exclude the possibilities of the formation of a customs union leading to the provision of more information about exchange possibilities within the union and to changes in consumers' preferences arising from the greater mingling of different national cultures. For our purposes here, however, the main concern about the assumptions underlying the demand function arises from the fact that they provide the basis for the analysis of the effects of the formation of a customs union on economic welfare. Given the one-to-one correspondence which links ss_x in figure 2.3 with the contract curve in figure 2.1, it can be seen that changes in the domestic terms of trade will result in movements along the contract curve with resulting changes in relative factor prices and hence relative factor incomes. In common with most trade and tariff theory, however, the basic approach of customs union theory has been to abstract from such distributional considerations in order to provide a unique measure of national economic welfare. This can be achieved by various sets of assumptions, all of which enable national economic welfare to be represented by a set of convex, non-intersecting community or social indifference curves drawn in commodity-space diagrams such as figure 2.2 as u, u' . . . The problem remains, however, of whether the essentially ordinal concept of welfare implied by such curves can be appropriately represented by quantity units of a commodity in diagrams such as figure 2.3. This problem has been the subject of a long debate in economics, but Burns (1973) has shown that the traditional measure of consumers' surplus is valid for models, like the present one, in which there is only one commodity price variable.[2]

Accordingly we can measure the gain in the y-value of consumer surplus for the change in the terms of trade from p' to p'' as $p'd'd''p''$ i.e. area (VII + I + III + II). Simultaneously, however, as we have already seen, the same price change reduces the y-value of income from production by $p's's''p''$, area (VII), so that the net gain in economic surplus is measured by $s'd'd''s''$, i.e. area (I + III + II). It can also be noted that, like the supply curve, the demand function drawn in figure 2.1 also provides information about demand for commodity y, as well as the more obvious information about demand for commodity x. Thus at p' the y-value of demand for x is $op'd'x'_d$ whilst at p'' it has changed to $op''d''x''_d$. Since the y-value of income has fallen by $p's's''p''$, i.e. area (VII), it follows that demand for y changes by the difference between $s'd'bs''$ and $x'_d bd''x''_d$, i.e. area (I + III – VI). From this, too, we can obtain a useful breakdown of the change in economic surplus. The change in the terms of trade allows consumers to reduce the amount of y they offer for the original quantity demanded of x by $p'd'bp''$, i.e. area (VII + I + III), though at the same time the y-value of their income falls by $p's's''p''$, i.e. area (VII). Thus, in addition to the original quantities of both x and y, consumers have available to them an extra amount of income measured in terms of y by $s'd'bs''$, area (I + III). This area can be split into two components. The rectangle $s'd'ba$, i.e. (III), represents the additional income which is available to the community as a result of the lower cost of the original volume of imports. This can be called the terms of trade effect. The triangle $s'as''$, i.e. (I), also represents

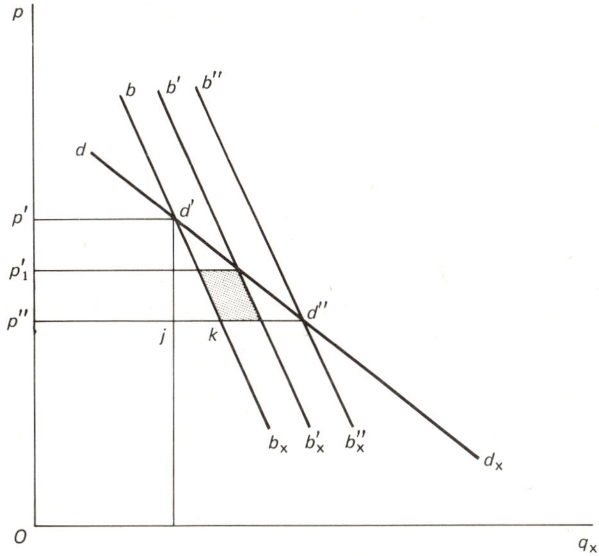

Figure 2.4 *Consumption Effects of a Price Change*

additional income available to the community, which as we have already seen results from the reaction of producers to the price change and the fact that the extra production of y is worth more at the terms of trade p' than the amount of x which it displaces. This can be termed the production effect. Similarly, however, consumers also react to the price change and, by increasing demand for x from x'_d to x''_d, obtain a gain which is measured in units of y by the triangle $d'bd''$, i.e. (II), and which can be termed the consumption effect.

Incidentally, all objections to the use of the cardinal measure of change in economic surplus are attributable solely to difficulties in interpreting and measuring this effect. Consider figure 2.4 which introduces Hicksian compensated demand curves, bb_x etc, in addition to the general equilibrium demand curve. As is well known, the area $p'd'kp''$ measures the (Hicksian) compensating variation in income for the fall in price from p' to p'', i.e. the y-value of the amount of income which can be withdrawn from the community whilst leaving welfare unaltered. Of this change, the area $p'd'jp''$ can be split into the changes in income from production and the production and terms of trade effects, the measurement of which raises no theoretical problems. The remaining component of the compensating variation in income is $d'kj$ and, if compensation was actually paid to maintain the initial level of welfare, this would measure the consumption effect. In most applications of tariff theory, however, there is no expectation that such compensation is paid. As a result, the Hicksian measure of the consumption effect will not only produce different measures for both directions of a price change which exactly reverses itself but will also produce different measures for any given price change, depending on the number of adjustment steps taken to accomplish it. Thus, if the change in the terms of trade is split into the fall from p' to p_1' and the fall from p_1' to p'', the sum of the producers' surplus, the production and the terms of trade effects attributable to the two steps is again $p'd'jp''$. The sum of the consumption effects on the other hand consists of the area $d'kj$ plus the shaded area in figure 2.2. By splitting the change in the terms of trade into still smaller parts, the estimate of the consumption effect will increase and approach the limit given by the area $d'd''j$. It is this limit which precisely measures the consumption effect employed here and which, unlike the Hicksian measure, equally measures the consumption effect of the price change from p'' to p'.

Figure 2.1 depicts the supply and demand conditions in the home country. For many problems, however, it is helpful to derive the foreign trade demand and/or supply functions. The derivation is accomplished with the simplifying assumptions that the costs of transport and of all other barriers to international trade is zero. This, of course, abstracts from the potentially important role of transport, which was recognised by the separate attention given to this in Articles 74–84 of the Treaty of Rome – see El-Agraa 1980, Chapter 8. For the present, however, this assumption enables us to depict the import demand function for commodity x as mm_x in figure 2.5. This function is constructed so that the lengths $p'm'$ and $p''m''$ are the same in figure 2.5 as the lengths $s'd'$ and $s''d''$ respectively in figure 2.3. In addition to showing the demand for imports of commodity x (e.g. x_m' at the terms of trade p'), the function also shows the supply of

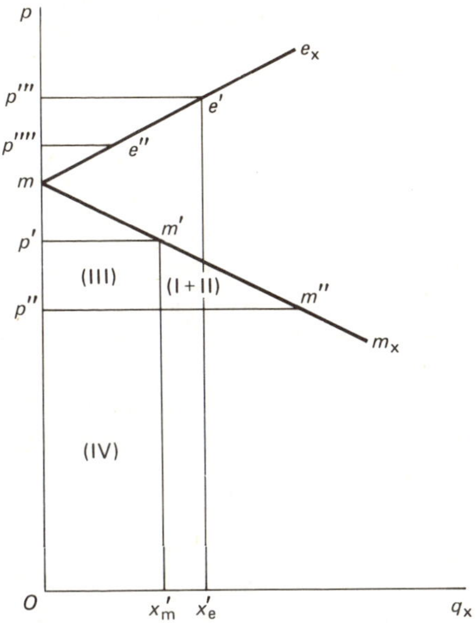

Figure 2.5 *Import Demand and Export Supply Conditions of the Home Country*

exports of commodity *y* offered in exchange, e.g. $op'm'x'_m$, i.e. area (III + IV), at the terms of trade p'. It also follows from the method of construction of the import demand function that the change in economic surplus due to any price change is measured by the area bounded by the appropriate price lines, the price axis and the import demand curve (so that, for example, $p'm'm''p''$ in figure 2.5 equals $s'd'd''s''$ in figure 2.3). It can also be noticed that, if the terms of trade rise above *m*, this economy would change from being an importer to being an exporter of *x*. Consequently, it is possible to obtain the export supply function me_x, which shows both the export supply of commodity *x*, e.g. x'_e at p''', and the quantity of imports of commodity *y* demanded in exchange, e.g. $op'''e'x'_e$ at p'''. In addition, as with the import demand function, this function can also be employed to depict changes in economic surplus due to a price change, so that, for example, the area $p'''e'e''p''''$ depicts the loss in economic welfare associated with the change in the terms of trade from p''' to p''''.

Traditional Customs Union Theory

To build a full model of a customs union it is necessary to depict the economies of at least two other 'countries', 'the partner' and 'the rest of the world'. Traditionally, however, much of customs union theory has avoided this complication by the introduction of the assumption that the home country is 'small' relative to the other two economies, so that its trade policies cannot alter the terms of trade offered by its trading partners. The apparent advantage provided by this assumption is that the formation of the customs union does not affect the terms of trade (and therefore economic welfare) in either of the other economies, so that the analysis need consider only the effects for the home country of joining the customs union.

This simple model is set out in figures 2.6 and 2.7, in which the home country's demand, supply and import demand functions for commodity x are identical with those shown in figures 2.3 and 2.5. The trading possibilities faced by the community are shown by the terms of trade offered by the

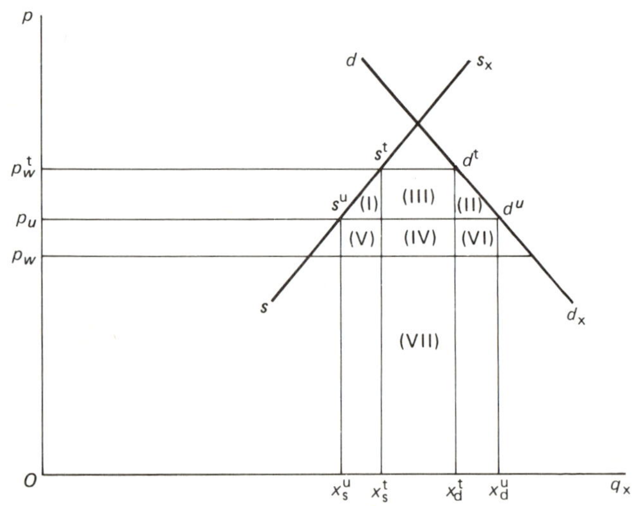

Figure 2.6

rest of the world and by the (potential) partner, p_w and p_u respectively. Prior to the formation of the customs union, the government of the home economy is assumed to levy the same (specific) tariff rate on all imports of commodity x so that the tariff-inclusive export supply curves of the foreign countries are shown by $p_w^t m^t$ and $p_u^t p_u^t$ respectively in figure 2.7. Consumers of x will, of course, wish to trade with the lowest cost suppliers of the commodity, so that the effective total supply function of commodity x is shown by $ss^t d^t$ in figure 2.6, whilst the effective foreign supply curve of imports is provided by the tariff-inclusive export supply curve of the rest of the world, i.e. $p_w^t m^t$ in figure 2.7 ($p_w^t s^t d^t$ in figure 2.6). In this situation domestic demand and supply of commodity x are shown as x_d^t and x_s^t, with import demand being shown as $x_s^t x_d^t$ in figure 2.6 (x_m^t in figure 2.7). In return for these imports, traders in the home country are prepared to offer exports of commodity y equal to $op_w^t m^t x_m^t$ in figure 2.7 ($x_s^t s^t d^t x_d^t$ in figure 2.6) but, of this offer, the government collects tariff revenue measured by the area (III + IV) in either diagram. In equilibrium, trade is exclusively with the

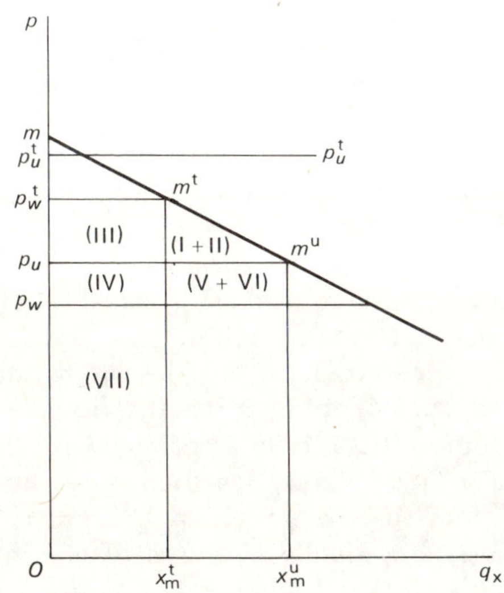

Figure 2.7

rest of the world and the quantity of y actually exported by the home country in exchange for imports of x_m^t is shown by area (VII).

The formation of a customs union between the home country and the partner requires the removal of the home country's tariffs on imports from the partner and the adoption of a tariff which is high enough to prohibit imports from the rest of the world. As a result of this change the effective supply curve facing consumers becomes $ss^u d^u$ in figure 2.6, whilst the effective foreign supply curve of imports is provided by the tariff-free export supply curve of the partner shown by $p_u s^u d^u$ in that figure and by $p_u m^u$ in figure 2.7. Domestic production of commodity x falls to x_s^u, whilst the increase in the domestic production of commodity y is measured by $x_s^t s^t s^u x_s^u$. Consumption of x increases to x_d^u as a result of an increase in the volume of imports from x_m^t $(x_s^t x_d^t)$ to x_m^u $(x_s^u x_d^u)$ and trade switches to being exclusively with the partner. As a result of the fall in the domestic terms of trade, the increase in the y-value of economic surplus is measured by area (I + II + III) but simultaneously tariff revenue, measured by area (III + IV), is eliminated. The y-value of net welfare effect is therefore shown as area (I + II – IV) and in general may be either positive or negative. We can see, however, that the increase in trade, $x_m^t x_m^u$ $(x_s^u x_s^t + x_d^t x_d^u)$ is associated with pure gain (I + II), whilst the original trade diverted from the rest of the world to the partner (x_m^t) is associated with the net loss shown by area (IV). It is this latter effect which corresponds to Viner's concept of trade diversion and which suggests that, in principle, the welfare loss associated with trade diversion can be measured by the volume of trade diverted multiplied by the difference between the terms of trade offered by the partner and the rest of the world. The increase in trade, $x_m^t x_m^u$, however, is not identical with Viner's concept of trade creation. This is because Viner ignored the consumption effect associated with the change in demand from x_d^t to x_d^u and identified only the production effect arising from the change in supply from x_s^t to x_s^u. Both effects, however, are equally a source of gain and we shall adopt the definition that trade creation consists of both the production and consumption effects.[3] In principle, the welfare gain associated with this may be measured and, even if the precise form of the import demand function is unknown, the gain may be approximated by the area of the triangle with base equal to the volume of trade created and height equal to the original tariff level.

Criticism of the Traditional Theory

These simple conclusions have remained very influential and have formed the basis of a number of empirical studies of schemes for economic integration – see El-Agraa 1980, Chapter 5. Indeed, a major implication of the analysis seemed to be that the merits of any scheme for economic integration required the evaluation of the trade creation and trade diversion effects. In 1965, however, Cooper and Massell 1965 showed that, even if the trade creation gain exceeded the trade diversion loss in economic welfare, this alone did not justify the formation of a customs union. The key to Cooper and Massell's approach lies in their introduction of an alternative policy choice involving the uniform reduction in the import tariff to the level at which the domestic terms of trade were identical to those which would result from membership of the customs union. In figures 2.6 and 2.7 the (specific) non-discriminatory tariff rate which has this effect is equal to $p_W p_u$ and, as a convenient shorthand hereafter, this tariff rate will be referred to as the alternative 'A' tariff.

With the introduction of this alternative policy choice, the welfare effects of joining a customs union can be compared with it as well as with the initial tariff policy. As can be seen from figures 2.6 and 2.7, since both the adoption of the 'A' tariff and membership of the customs union result in the same fall in the internal terms of trade (to p_u), both policies have identical effects on consumption, production and the volume of trade. Accordingly, both policies also bring identical changes in economic surplus – the gains shown by areas (I + II + III). Indeed, the only difference between them is that, whereas, with the non-discriminatory policy, trade continues to be with the rest of the world, with membership of the customs union, trade is diverted to being with the partner. Accordingly, membership of the customs union yields no tariff revenue (and hence a loss shown by area (III + IV) compared to the initial position), whereas, with the non-preferential tariff reduction, tariff revenue shown by area (IV + V + VI) is obtained. Compared to the initial tariff, the adoption of the 'A' rate therefore involves the net change in tariff revenue shown as area (V + VI − III) which, when combined with the change in economic surplus resulting from the tariff change, shows the net welfare effect to be one of unambiguous gain which consists partly of a production effect, area (I + V), and partly of a consumption effect, area (II + VI). More significantly, the adoption of the 'A' tariff is also revealed as unambiguously superior to membership of the customs union because of the differences in tariff revenue associated with the two policies. Indeed, from the viewpoint of the home country, the welfare effects of membership of a customs union can be regarded as being equivalent to (i) the net welfare effect of moving from the initial tariff to the 'A' rate, i.e. (I + V + II + VI), plus (ii) the inevitable welfare loss associated with foregoing the tariff revenue which would have been obtained if the alternative, 'A' policy, had been adopted, i.e. (IV + V + VI). As with the Vinerian approach, these two components of the welfare effects of membership of a customs union are associated with the volume of trade created and the volume of trade diverted respectively. They do not correspond exactly with the Vinerian concepts of trade creation and trade diversion and, since Cooper and Massell also use the term trade diversion to describe (ii), it is important to recognise the difference between the two definitions. As can be seen from either figure 2.6 or figure 2.7, the Vinerian measure (area IV) is based on the pre-union volume of trade whereas Cooper and Massell's definition (area IV + V + VI) relates to the (potential) post-union volume of trade. Both measures have their uses and we shall see in Chapter 5 that the Vinerian concept is of value when terms of trade effects are also considered but in the present context it is undoubtedly Cooper and Massell's definition which points to the more powerful result. Whether or not the Vinerian trade diversion loss outweighs the trade creation gain of moving from the initial tariff to membership of a customs union, the latter cannot be regarded as a rational policy choice since Cooper and Massell's trade diversion effect shows that it is unambiguously inferior to the alternative policy of an appropriate uniform change in the import tariff.

This argument may appear to support the conclusion of Krauss 1972 (p. 434) that customs unions are the product of 'irrational' government action and that the economist's sole task in addition to emphasising this simple point should be to conduct empirical investigations to identify the economic costs involved. Such a conclusion, however, must be regarded as premature. Despite its influential nature, the traditional (Vinerian) analysis is based on extremely restrictive assumptions and can best be regarded as a special case of the general model developed to sustain the case for a policy of free trade – a policy which, as can readily be checked from figures 2.6 and 2.7, is optimal for the home country. Thus, the main implication of Cooper and Massell's analysis is that it is necessary to widen the scope of the basic theory if we are to find an explanation for the formation of a customs union.

Variations within the Traditional Approach to Customs Union Theory

One way forward from this latter conclusion may be to investigate whether the results so far obtained from the standard version of the basic model are equally applicable when alternative assumptions about cost and demand conditions are considered. Such alternatives are, in fact, widely represented in the literature of the traditional approach to customs union theory but, rather than attempt to trace the development of this literature, the intention here is to provide only a summary of the results for the six main versions which can be identified. Within each version a number of different tariff policy alternatives can be considered. These are identified as follows (with common notation for figures 2.8, 2.9 and 2.10, all of which incorporate p^u and p^w as the given terms of trade offered by the partner and the rest of the world respectively):

(A) the non-discriminatory (and non-prohibitive) tariff $p^{w}p^{u}$ which leaves the home country with exactly the same domestic terms of trade as does membership of a customs union formed with the partner economy;
(B) any arbitrary non-prohibitive non-discriminatory tariff, represented in all the diagrams by $p^{w}p^{t}$;
(C) the (minimal) prohibitive (non-discriminatory) tariff, represented in all the diagrams by $p^{w}p'$;
(D) membership of a customs union formed with the partner economy and involving the two steps (i) the removal of the existing tariff on imports from the partner, and (ii) the establishment of a common external tariff of sufficient height to prohibit trade with the rest of the world; and
(E) the policy of free trade which could, from the home country's viewpoint, equally be regarded as the formation of a customs union with the rest of the world rather than with the 'partner'.

This then enables us to tabulate the results of six different kinds of policy change for each version of the theory:

(1) the change from policy B to policy D, which has been the main focus of the traditional literature and which unfortunately has frequently been misleadingly labelled as the case of a 'trade-diverting customs union' (see Johnson 1974);
(2) the change from policy C to policy D, which is also examined in the traditional literature under the label of a 'trade-creating customs union';
(3) the change from policy A to policy D, following the suggestion of Cooper and Massell, with the implication that the effects of non-discriminatory tariff reductions should also be identified; so that we consider
(4) the change from policy B to policy A (i.e. a lowering in the level of a non-prohibitive tariff);
(5) the change from policy C to policy A (i.e. a move from a prohibitive to a non-prohibitive tariff); and
(6) the change from policy A to policy E (i.e. the elimination of any effective tariff barrier either by the adoption of

universal free trade or else the formation of a customs union with the lowest cost source of importables, i.e. the rest of the world).

(i) The Case of Constant Costs and Constant Demand

It was this particularly simplified version of the model, which is set out in figure 2.8 with the domestic demand curve $x_d d_x$ and domestic supply curve $p' s_x$, which prompted the use of the labels 'trade-diverting' and 'trade-creating' customs unions as applying to the policy changes examined in columns (1) and (2) of table 2.1. In this case no ambiguity does arise with these labels. Policy change (1) is shown to involve only pure trade diversion loss, whilst policy change (2) is equally shown to involve only pure trade creation gain. Cooper and Massell's approach, however, shows that such a policy change (2) is still not justified, given the alternative policy change of a non-discriminatory reduction in the tariffs to the A rate. Compared to this policy, membership of the customs union (as in all the cases considered below) produces only pure trade diversion loss.

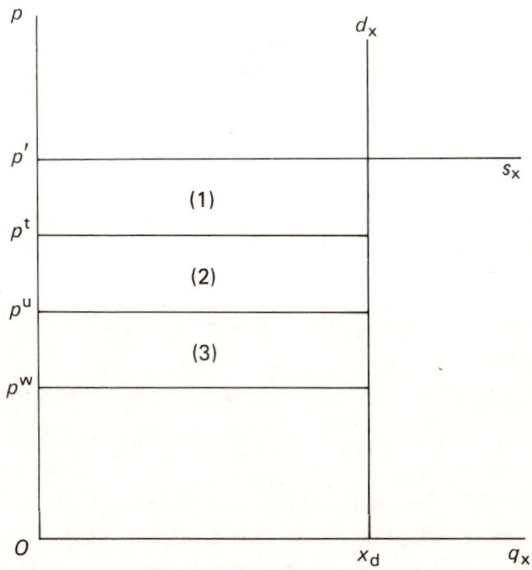

Figure 2.8 *The Traditional Model: the Case of Constant Costs and Constant Demand.*

Table 2.1 *Tariff Policy Changes in the Cases of Constant or Decreasing Costs with Constant Demand (see figures 2.8 and 2.10)*

Resource Realloca-tion Effects	*Policy Change* (1) B→D	(2) C→D	(3) A→D	(4) B→A	(5) C→A	(6) A→E
(i) Tariff revenue	−(2+3)	0	−(3)	−(2)	+(3)	−(3)
(ii) Domestic terms of trade	+(2)	0	0	+(2)	0	+(3)
(iii) Trade diversion[1]	−(3)	0	−(3)			
(iv) Production	0	+(1+2)	0	0	+(1+2)	0
(v) Consumption	0	0	0	0	0	0
(vi) Trade creation[2]	0	+(1+2)	0	0	+(1+2+3)	0
(vii) Total	−(3)	+(1+2)	−(3)	0	+(1+2+3)	0

Notes: 1 & 2 See notes for table 2.2

(ii) The Case of Constant Costs and Variable Demand

This version of the model differs from the previous one only in so far as all the policy changes which involve a fall in the domestic terms of trade, i.e. all those tabulated except that in column (3), result in a consumption effect gain. This has the effect of destroying the validity of labelling policy change (1) as the formation of a purely trade-diverting customs union and also establishes the clear superiority of policy E over all other policy choices. Cooper and Massell's lesson continues to apply. Whether or not policy change (1) can be shown to involve net gain, like policy change (2), it is still inferior to the policy of non-discriminatory tariff reduction, compared to which, as policy change (3) shows, the formation of a customs union with the partner results solely in a trade diversion loss.

(iii) The Case of Increasing Costs and Constant Demand

The version of the model is shown in figure 2.9 and the results are summarised in table 2.2. The assumption of constant demand again rules out all consumption effects but (unlike in either the constant cases above or the decreasing cost cases below) changes involving non-prohibitive tariffs,

Table 2.2 *Tariff Policy Changes in the Case of Increasing Costs and Constant Demand* (see figure 2.9)

Resource Reallocation Effects	*Policy Change* (1) B→D	(2) C→D	(3) A→D	(4) B→A	(5) C→A	(6) A→E
(i) Tariff revenue	−(2+3)	0	−(3+5)	(5−2)	+(3+5)	−(3+5)
(ii) Domestic terms of trade	+(2)	0	0	+(2)	0	+(3+5)
(iii) Trade diversion[1]	−(3)	0	−(3+5)	—	—	—
(iv) Production	+(4)	+(1+2+4)	0	+(4)	+(1+2+4)	+(6)
(v) Consumption	0	0	0	0	0	0
(vi) **Trade creation**[2]	+(4)	+(1+2+4)	0	+(4+5)	+(1+2+3+4+5)	+(6)
(vii) Total	(4−3)	+(1+2+4)	−(3+5)	+(4+5)	+(1+2+3+4+5)	+(6)

Notes: 1 This employs the definition that trade diversion is the sum of the effects of (i) and (ii) in the three cases (1), (2) and (3), involving the formation of a customs union.

2 For cases (1), (2) and (3), this is based on the definition that trade creation is equal to the sum of the production and consumption effects. For cases (4), (5) and (6) it also incorporates the net outcome of (i) and (ii) and is sometimes termed the tariff reduction effect (see Cooper and Massell 1965).

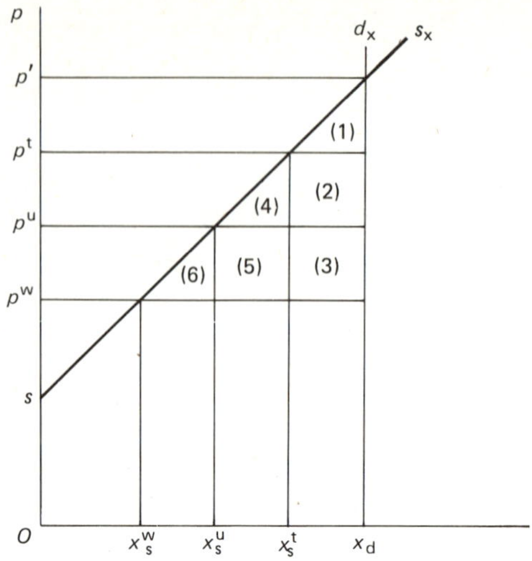

Figure 2.9 *The Traditional Model: the Case of Increasing Costs and Constant Demand.*

i.e. (1), (3), (4) and (6), all result in a positive production effect gain. As with the consumption effect in the previous case, this destroys the validity of labelling policy change (1) as the formation of a purely trade-diverting customs union and equally provides a source of the superiority of policy E over all other policy choices.

(iv) The Case of Increasing Costs and Variable Demand

This is the standard version of the model already analysed in terms of figures 2.6 and 2.7. The results are identical in effect to those in table 2.2 (though the numbering of the areas is not the same as that used in the earlier diagrams) with the exception that positive consumption effects would again be present in all columns except (3).

(v) The Case of Decreasing Costs and Constant Demand

This case seems to have received least attention and is different from those considered earlier in that the assumption of perfect competition conditions in the commodity market

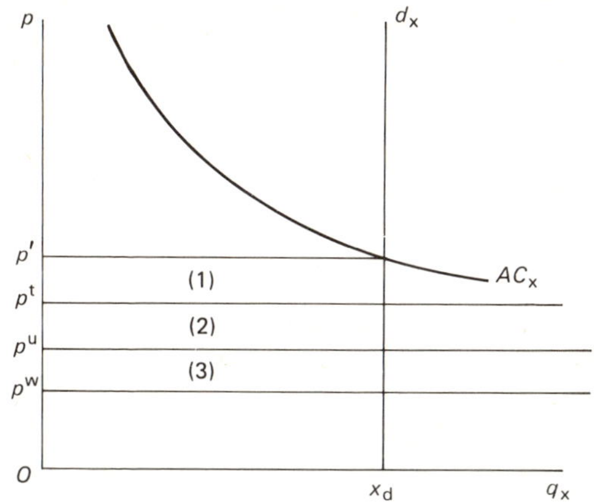

Figure 2.10 *The Traditional Model: the Case of Decreasing Costs and Constant Demand.*

seems inappropriate, so that the inverse of the marginal cost curve can no longer be regarded as the supply function. This problem, however, can be surmounted by the use of the average (opportunity) cost curve AC_x in figure 2.10, which can be obtained directly from the marginal cost curve, and by the assumption that production is controlled by a profit-maximising monopolist. It then follows that domestic production of importables will occur only if the domestic price level is sufficient to cover the monopolist's costs. The minimum tariff which will achieve this result has been called the 'made-to-measure' tariff (see Corden 1972) and is depicted in figure 2.10 by the rate $p^w p'$, i.e. by tariff policy C. This is, of course, a prohibitive tariff, whilst all lower tariffs, as in the cases of constant costs, are purely revenue devices since they have no protective effect and allow imports to capture the entire home market. Consequently, only the changes from policy C (i.e. columns 2 and 5) involve a production effect and the comparisons of alternative policy changes yield identical results to case (i), which are summarised in table 2.1.

(vi) The Case of Decreasing Costs and Variable Demand

The replacement of the assumption of constant demand by

that of variable demand simply has the effect of again introducing consumption effect gains for all the policy changes which result in a reduction in the domestic terms of trade. Thus the conclusions of case (ii) are equally applicable here.

These results suggest that, in all cases, the main conclusion to be drawn seems to be that first pointed to by Cooper and Massell. If the formation of a customs union is compared with an arbitrary initial tariff, it may either increase or decrease economic welfare, depending on the relative strengths of the trade creation and trade diversion effects it brings about. Whatever the result of such a comparison, however, when the formation of a customs union is compared with the non-discriminatory tariff reduction to the level of policy A, it can be seen to involve only pure trade diversion loss. Of course, the formation of a customs union with the lowest cost source of imports is unambiguously trade-creating and welfare-increasing, but this merely reflects the equivalence of such a policy with that of the simpler unilateral adoption by the home country of a free trade policy.

It therefore seems necessary to go beyond what can only be regarded as equivalent to the first stage of development in tariff theory (as identified by Corden 1974) to apply the methods of optimal intervention analysis to the problem of explaining the formation of a customs union.

Notes

1 This terminology can be misleading. If the same consequences of the price change had been measured in units of x, they would have revealed an increase in the x-value of domestic production and thus a gain in the equally valid x-value measure of producer's surplus. It should also be realised that the model does not distinguish between two distinct groups, 'producers' and 'consumers', and that in order to evaluate the effects of the price change it is necessary to take into account the simultaneous effect that this has on the market condition facing consumers. It is only the net outcome of the two simultaneous effects which is important and, providing the *numéraire* is used consistently, both the x-value measure and the y-value measure of the net outcome will yield identical results.

2 It should be noted that the validity of the measure does not require either that zero income elasticities of demand are assumed or that dd_x is a Hicksian compensated demand curve. The demand curve dd_x is simply the counterpart in figure 2.3 of the offer/price consumption curve which could have been obtained by joining together points such as C' and C'' in figure 2.2. The validity of the measure flows instead from the definition of consumers surplus as the limit of the sum of compensating variations in income for any change in the terms of trade treated as a series of infinitesimally small adjustments. Although in general such a measure is not well-defined, it is for the present model, as the existence of only a single price variable implies that the path of price adjustments is unique for any given change in the terms of trade (see below pp. 17–18).

3 Unfortunately there is no unanimity in the literature on the appropriate definition of trade creation and, in addition to the usage suggested, other writers have preferred to restrict the term trade creation to Viner's definition whilst adding new terms such as 'trade expansion' for the consumption effect (Meade 1956) or 'gross trade creation' for the production and consumption effects combined (Balassa 1967).

3

Customs Unions versus Free Trade Areas

A M EL-AGRAA

The theory of economic integration has paid very little attention to the differences between customs unions (CUs) and free trade areas (FTAs). (Bela Balassa (1962) devotes a few pages to some of the basic issues; V. Curzon (1974) examines some of the differences; H. Shibata (1967) discusses the implications of 'rules of origin' for free trade areas). In purely definitional terms, the only difference between the two types of economic union is the adoption of a common external tariff (CET) in a CU. (In both customs unions and free trade areas, members remove all impediments on mutual trade. However, in a free trade area members retain their freedom to determine their extra-union commercial policies. Needless to say, this freedom is denied to members of a customs union.) The purpose of this chapter is to examine the basic concepts employed in this field in a manner that makes it possible to investigate differences between CUs and FTAs so as to highlight certain aspects of customs unions.

The Differences

The difference between a CU and a FTA with respect to the external tariff rates leads to certain complications. These are clearly expressed in a proposition advanced by Professor Balassa:

> . . . the maintenance of differing tariff rates of duties in trade with non-participating countries will create possibilities for *deflection of trade, production, and investment*. Deflection of trade will occur if the trade barriers of high-tariff member countries are circumvented through the importation of products originating outside the area from low-tariff members. If no precautionary measures were taken and tariff differentials exceeded the additional costs of transportation, imports would enter the free-trade area via the country which applies the lowest tariff on the commodity in question . . .
>
> Besides causing deflection of trade, the establishment of a free-trade area may bring about an uneconomic structure of production. The manufacture of products which *contain a high percentage of foreign-made materials and semi-finished products will shift to low-tariff countries if differences in tariffs outweigh differences in production* . . . The ensuing reallocation of resources will have detrimental effects on world efficiency since the pattern of productive activity will not follow the lines of comparative advantage but rather the difference in duties.
>
> Deflection of production may also be accompanied by undesirable movements of capital funds. The establishment of so-called tariff factories is a case in point; other things being equal, foreign investors will move funds to countries with lower tariffs on raw materials and semi-manufactured products. Similarly, factories will be set up to assemble parts produced in third countries with low labour costs if tariff advantages make this operation possible. (Balassa 1962, pp. 70–71. The emphasis is not in the original text.)

Before I proceed to examine Balassa's proposition in some detail, let me first discuss the concepts of trade creation, trade diversion and trade deflection in a manner that makes it easy to distinguish between customs unions and free trade areas.

Trade Creation

Consider a situation where the following conditions hold initially:

$$P_1 < P_3 (1 + t_1) \quad (1)$$
$$P_1 < P_2 (1 + t_1) \quad (2)$$
$$P_2 < P_3 (1 + t_2) \quad (3)$$
$$P_2 < P_1 (1 + t_2) \quad (4)$$

where: P is the unit price of a particular commodity; 1, 2, 3 are the three exclusive and mutually exhaustive areas of the world, with 1 and 2 as the potential integration partners and 3 as the rest of the world (W); and t is the *ad valorem* tariff duty levied on imported finished products.

The first and the second conditions ensure that country 1 is producing enough to satisfy its domestic demand, i.e. its tariff rate is prohibitive. The third and fourth conditions ensure the same outcome for country 2.

When countries 1 and 2 form a FTA, they maintain their initial tariff rates on imports from 3, but abolish them for mutual trade. Assuming that $P_1 > P_2 > P_3$, the first and third conditions will still hold true. However, since $P_2 < P_1$, country 1 will now give up the production of this commodity and import it from its partner. This is trade creation: a lower cost FTA partner is substituted for the higher cost home producers without having any repercussions on W. (See Chapter 2 for a more specific definition.) Alternative assumptions either do not affect this outcome ($P_1 > P_3 > P_2$; $P_3 > P_1 > P_2$), or make country 1 the recipient of the gains from trade creation ($P_2 > P_1 > P_3$; $P_2 > P_3 > P_1$; $P_3 > P_2 > P_1$) given the appropriate specification of the conditions.

If, instead of forming a FTA, countries 1 and 2 decide to establish a CU they will have to adopt a CET, as well as abolish tariffs on their mutual trade. Let us assume that the CET is set equal to the unweighted arithmetical average of the initial tariff rates, i.e. $[(t_1 + t_2)/2 = t']$.

Now, if t_1 is initially equal to t_2, there is no difference between a CU and FTA. However, if t_1 is initially higher than t_2, t_2 must rise as a consequence of the adoption of a CET. Hence, the third condition will still hold true – country 2 will still not import from W. At the same time, t_1 must fall. The question arises as to whether t_1 will fall to such an extent as to reverse condition (1) $[P_1 > P_3(1 - t')]$, because if such a situation were to arise, country 1 would import this commodity from W. Since P_2 is less than $P_3(1 + t)$[1] and less than P_1, P_2 can never be higher than $P_3(1 + t')$ at the same time. Hence the only possible outcome is that country 1 will import this commodity from country 2 after the formation of the CU.

If t_1 is initially lower than t_2, t_1 must rise whilst t_2 must fall as a result of the adoption of a CET. When t_1 rises, condition (1) will still hold true. Since $P_2 < P_1$, country 1 will import the commodity from country 2 provided, of course, that P_2 does not exceed $P_3(1 + t')$. Hence the only possible outcome is that neither country 1 nor country 2 will import this commodity from *W*; country 2 will capture the CU market. This is trade creation.

Trade Diversion

Now consider the case where the following conditions hold initially:

$$P_1 > P_3(1 + t_1) \qquad (4)$$
$$P_1 < P_2(1 + t_1) \qquad (2)$$
$$P_2 < P_3(1 + t_2) \qquad (3)$$

Conditions (2) and (4) ensure that country 1 is importing this commodity from *W* initially, whilst condition (3) guarantees that country 2 has a prohibitive tariff rate with respect to imports from *W*.

When countries 1 and 2 establish a FTA, both conditions (4) and (3) will still hold true. If one assumes that $P_1 > P_2$, country 1 will start importing this commodity from country 2 (instead of from *W*), but only if $P_2 < P_3(1 + t_1)$. If $t_1 \geqslant t_2$ this condition is readily satisfied by implication – condition (3). If, however, $t_1 < t_2$, there is a possibility that country 1 may continue to import from *W*; this possibility clearly depends on the extent of the tariff rate differential. Apart from this exception, here is a clear case of trade diversion: the substitution of cheap initial imports from *W* for more expensive imports from the FTA partner ($P_2 > P_3$). (See Chapter 2 for a more specific definition.)

If however, $P_1 < P_2$, country 1 will still continue to import from *W*, i.e. the FTA will have no effect as far as this commodity is concerned.

If countries 1 and 2 form a CU rather than a FTA, there will be no difference (CU *versus* FTA) if $t_1 = t_2$ initially, assuming that $P_2 < P_1$. If $t_1 < t_2$ initially, t_1 must rise and t_2 must fall to the CET level. When this happens, t_1 may rise to such a level as to reverse condition (4). In such circumstances t_2 cannot fall to such an extent as to reverse condition (3), since this would imply that $P_2 > P_1$, which is ruled out by assumption. Hence condition (3) must still hold true.

The reversing of condition (4) means that country 1 will no longer import this commodity from *W*. Since $P_2 < P_1$, country 1 will now import this commodity from country 2, the FTA partner. This is a clear case of trade diversion.

If subjecting t_1 and t_2 to a CET does not lead to a reversal of either condition (4) or (3), trade diversion will still take place particularly since $P_1 > P_3(1 + t')$, $P_2 < P_3(1 + t')$ and $P_2 < P_1$.

A more interesting outcome is where a higher t_1 does not reverse condition (4) but the lower t_2 reverses condition (3). In such circumstances, country 1 will continue to import from *W* and country 2 will now give up its costly domestic production and import from *W*. This is external trade creation, a phenomenon which can only occur in the case of CU formation.

If $t_1 > t_2$ initially, t_1 must fall and t_2 must rise in order to achieve a CET. In such circumstances conditions (4) and (3) will always hold true. Since $P_2 < P_3(1 + t')$ and $P_1 > P_2$, the only possible outcome is that country 1 will start importing this commodity from country 2 instead of from *W*. This is therefore the clearest case of trade diversion: the higher cost potential partner has the higher tariff rate initially. In Corden's terms,[2] trade diversion is the only possible outcome when tariffs are 'made to measure'.

Trade Deflection

It is possible that both countries 1 and 2 are importing a commodity initially. In such circumstances, the following conditions must be satisfied:

$$P_1 > P_3(1 + t_1) \qquad (4)$$
$$P_2 > P_3(1 + t_2) \qquad (5)$$

Because of these initial conditions, the assumption that $P_1 \geqslant P_2$ has no significance at this stage. Of course, the calculation of P_1 and P_2 is hypothetical in these circumstances.

Assuming that $t_1 > t_2$, the price of this commodity in country 1 will exceed the price in country 2. It is apparent that country 1 could not have been importing this commodity via country 2, particularly since $[P_3(1 + t_2)]\ (1 + t_1)$ is obviously in excess of $P_3(1 + t_1)$. Hence both countries must be importing *directly* from W.

When countries 1 and 2 enter into a FTA, country 1 will import this commodity via country 2, provided the price differential exceeds the necessary transportation charges and provided that there are no 'rules of origin'[3] to exclude this possibility. This phenomenon is referred to as 'deflection of trade' (the term is coined by Balassa 1962, p. 70): the country that initially imported a commodity *directly* from W now imports it *indirectly* via the partner with the lower tariff rate.

If, however, countries 1 and 2 establish a CU, t_1 will have to fall and t_2 will have to rise in order to have a CET. In such circumstances the price of this commodity will be the same in both countries i.e. $[P_1 = P_2 = P_3(1 + t')]$. Hence both countries will continue to import this commodity directly from W.

If $t_1 = t_2$ initially, then of course there is no difference between a CU and a FTA.

Comparisons and Conclusion

In spite of the fact that the above analysis is based on highly restrictive assumptions, e.g. constant prices, one can still make some comparisons between CUs and FTAs. With regard to trade creation, there does not seem to be any fundamental difference between the two types of economic union. If there *is* any difference, it is likely to be one of magnitude, e.g. the effect of changing tariff rates in a CU on the volume of trade.

As far as trade diversion is concerned, however, there is a possibility that the adoption of a CET may lead to external trade creation in circumstances which might lead to trade diversion in a FTA. This is by no means a remote possibility, since the requirement of irrational tariff levels cannot be readily discarded. In this respect, a CU is superior to a FTA.

Trade deflection is a phenomenon peculiar to FTAs. If there exist no 'rules of origin', a FTA will produce a CET equal to the minimum tariff rate within the union. If this were the case, then a FTA would be superior to a CU; this conclusion and its implications are rigorously demonstrated by Curzon in a book which deals extensively with some of the problems of FTAs (Curzon 1974, Chapter 10).

Overall, one can argue that since most existing FTAs seem to have some sort of 'rules of origin', and since we have no evidence that tariffs are 'made to measure', it seems that the formation of a CU should be more encouraged than the establishment of a FTA. This conclusion is reinforced if one takes into consideration the other phenomena of deflection of production and investment in FTAs, to which I now turn.

Deflection of Production and Investment

Deflection of production, unaccompanied by deflection of investment, can occur only if both countries 1 and 2 are producing the same commodity initially. Moreover, it is necessary to assume the existence of excess capacity in the particular commodity in the country to which production is to be deflected; otherwise, expenditure on additional fixed capital equipment will become necessary and this would obviously represent a deflection of investment.

The assumption concerning the existence of excess capacity undoubtedly raises the problem of the effect of increased (decreased) level of output on the marginal and average costs of production. I shall ignore this problem at this stage for reasons that will become apparent shortly.

For both countries 1 and 2 to have been producing the same commodity prior to the formation of the FTA, the following conditions need to have been satisfied simultaneously in the initial situation:

$$P_2 < P_1 \qquad \text{(i)}$$

$$P_2(1 + t_1) > P_1 \qquad \text{(ii)}$$

Condition (i) specifies that country 2 is more efficient than country 1, hence there is no need for country 2 to impose a tariff duty on country 1. Condition (ii) ensures that country 1 has a prohibitive tariff rate. The conditions also imply that *W* either does not produce this product, or does not trade in it. (One could introduce further inequalities to ensure this result, but it is obvious that such conditions would be redundant.)

Let us assume that the price of this commodity is determined by the marginal (equals the average) cost[4] of production and that this cost is composed of two elements: the cost of domestic materials inclusive of all payments to the domestic factors employed per unit of extra output ($q \cdot p^*$ where p^* is the factor price and q is the physical quantity), and the cost of imported raw materials ($q \cdot p_3^*$ where p_3 is the price of raw materials charged by *W* and q is the physical quantity of imported raw materials). It therefore follows that:

$$P_1 = q_1 \cdot p_1^* + q_1^* \cdot p_3^* \, (1 + t_1^*) \qquad \text{(iii)}$$

$$P_2 = q_2 \cdot p_2^* + q_2^* \cdot p_3^* \, (1 + t_2^*) \qquad \text{(iv)}$$

where t^* is the *ad valorem* tariff duty on imported raw materials and semi-manufactured goods.

Let us assume that the physical quantities of factor imports are the same for both countries. Then the price definitions become:

$$P_1 = q \cdot p_1^* + q^* \cdot p_3^* \, (1 + t_1^*) \qquad \text{(iii}'\text{)}$$

$$P_2 = q \cdot p_2^* + q^* \cdot P_3^* \, (1 + t_2^*) \qquad \text{(iv}'\text{)}$$

It is of course more realistic to assume that an imported raw material for one country is a domestic raw material for another. Such an assumption, realistic as it may be, will obscure the whole issue and will make complete nonsense of Balassa's proposition. The case where the prices of the imported raw materials are different is discussed in a later section.

At this point it is necessary to establish that there is in fact a comparative cost advantage. This obviously cannot be taken to refer to the price charged for imported raw materials or to their physical quantities. If there is any advantage it must be entirely due to a tariff differential. I shall follow Balassa and assume that $t_1^* > t_2^*$. If there exists any true comparative cost advantage it must, therefore, relate to the domestic costs of production.

It is implicit in the price definitions that the commodity is produced under the same technological conditions in both countries. A true comparative cost advantage in country 1 must mean that $q \cdot p_1^* < q \cdot p_2^*$. Since the physical quantity is the same, then the cost advantage must refer to a factor price differential, i.e. $p_1^* < p_2^*$.

This point might require further explanation. In order to avoid the existence of any comparative cost advantage regarding imported raw materials except for the tariff differential, the physical quantities of these materials must be the same for both countries. Since it is assumed that this commodity is subject to the same production function, it follows that the physical quantity of domestic materials must also be the same per unit of output for both countries. The only difference is that the price per unit of domestic materials must be lower in country 1 than in country 2.

Admittedly, this implies that the production function exhibits fixed coefficients of production, i.e. the elasticity of substitution between foreign and domestic inputs per unit of this commodity is equal to zero.[5] But this is unavoidable if comparative cost advantage is to be meaningful in this particular context. Otherwise, if each country substitutes more of the relatively cheaper factor for the relatively dearer one, country 1 will employ more domestic materials and less imported materials. Country 2 will substitute in the opposite direction. This substitution will continue until the cost of production is the same in both countries (after the formation of a FTA).

The final outcome of such substitution is that the initial input composition necessary for producing a unit of this commodity becomes different in the two countries. This by no means suggests that production will be curtailed in country 1 and expanded in country 2, unless the total demand for this commodity changes in such a way as to bring this result about. In such circumstances the change in the production pattern has *nothing to do with supply conditions.* There is, therefore, no plausible reason why such a phenomenon should be associated with Balassa's proposition; it is simply a natural factor substitution situation in its simplest possible (textbook) form.

Establishment of a FTA

When countries 1 and 2 establish a FTA, they abolish their tariff rates of duty on inter-area trade in finished products ($t_1 = 0$) and maintain their external tariff rates on finished products, raw materials and semi-manufactured products coming from W, ($t_1^* > t_2^*$). It is then apparent from (i) and (ii) that country 1 will cease production of this commodity and that country 2 will take over its entire production.

Let us examine this situation closely. Substituting the definitional equations (iii′) and (iv′) into (i) gives:

$$q \cdot p_2^* + q^* \cdot p_3^* (1 + t_2^*) < q \cdot p_1^* + q^* \cdot p_3^* (1 + t_1^*)$$

Rearranging and simplifying gives:

$$q(p_2^* - p_1^*) < q^* \cdot p_3^* (t_1^* - t_2^*) \quad \text{(v)}$$

It is obvious that if this condition is fulfilled, then the domestic cost difference must fall short of the imported cost difference, the latter being entirely due to the tariff differential. This condition, therefore, states more precisely Balassa's proposition that deflection of production will take place when the tariff differential advantage exceeds the comparative cost disadvantage taking into account transport costs. It must be emphasised, however, that the tariff rates of duty referred to are those imposed on semi-manufactured goods and raw materials, *not tariffs on finished commodities.*

Let me be more precise about what condition (v) actually specifies. It states that for any given ratio of domestic materials to imported raw materials and semi-finished goods (q/q^*) and given the import price of these intermediate goods (p_3^*), the higher (lower) the factor price differential ($p_2^* - p_1^*$), the lower (higher) the tariff differential ($t_1^* - t_2^*$) that is necessary to ensure that deflection of production and investment will take place. Expressed differently, for any given factor price differential, intermediate imported goods price and tariff rate differential, the higher (lower) the ratio of imported intermediate goods to domestic materials, the more (less) is the likelihood of deflection of production and investment, which is Balassa's way of expressing it.

Constant Costs

It is now important to discuss the significance of omitting the crucial relationship between optimum output and minimum costs. The justification is that if, as country 2 expands its production of this commodity, the marginal cost (equal to the average) falls to such an extent as to make the cost of production the same in both countries, then the term comparative cost advantage will become devoid of any meaning. In order to make any sense of the term one has to assume that even if country 2's industry were to operate at an optimum level, its marginal cost would still be higher than country 1's. In other words, even if it is assumed that the optimum level of production and the optimum plant size are exactly the same in both countries, and even if these were actually realised in both countries, country 1 would still produce at a lower marginal cost of production, i.e. the only difference would be due to a factor price differential.

If deflection of investment were also to occur, the marginal cost calculations could be affected in two opposing ways. Firstly, the expenditure on fixed capital equipment, particularly if it is not expected to have a long life, would raise the cost calculations. Secondly, the newly acquired fixed capital might be technologically more advanced (economically more efficient) thus leading to lower cost calculations overall. Bearing in mind the argument of the previous paragraph, it must again be assumed that the net result of these counteracting forces would leave the domestic cost differential intact. Otherwise the term comparative cost advantage must be given a dynamic interpretation, in which case Balassa's proposition becomes completely meaningless.

Only One Country Producing the Commodity

If country 1 had been the only country producing this commodity before the formation of the FTA, the following condition must have been satisfied:

$$P_1\ (1 + t_2) < P_2 \qquad \text{(vi)}$$

This is the reverse of condition (ii) and it ensures that either country 2 is not consuming this commodity at all, or is importing it from its potential FTA partner. Since this commodity is not produced at all in country 2 initially, the cost calculations are subject to the difficulties regarding hypothetical estimates. (J.E. Meade (1955) gives a taxonomic approach for calculating costs under such circumstances.) It is assumed that such calculations can be accurately made.

The condition that must necessarily be satisfied in order that production should be deflected to country 2 after the formation of a FTA is:

$$P_2 < P_1 \qquad \text{(vii)}$$

subject to the reservation regarding hypothetical cost calculations and that condition (vi) is satisfied prior to the formation of the FTA.

It is quite obvious that if (vi) is fulfilled (with positive tariffs), (vii) will *never* be satisfied: if P_2 exceeds $P_1\ (1 + t_2)$, it can never be less than P_1!

Note that when structural changes are being considered, production costs and investment calculations must be made simultaneously. Hence, neither deflection of production nor deflection of investment can occur when only one country is producing a commodity initially. If tariff rates were negative (i.e. subsidies), then Balassa's proposition would make no sense at all: either a country's comparative cost advantage is reinforced or its domestic cost disadvantage is negated!

With regard to this case, the analysis has been conducted on the assumption that country 1 is producing the commodity initially. However, the analysis could very well be conducted on the assumption that country 2 is producing the commodity initially. The conclusion is of course still the same, in that it would not be possible for country 1 to take over the production of this commodity.

What is the implication of this? If country 1 has a true comparative cost advantage in producing this commodity, then in the case when it is the only country producing the commodity initially, country 2 will never be able to compete when a FTA is established. However, when only country 2 is producing the commodity initially, no deflection is possible, even though country 1 has a true comparative advantage. This seems to suggest an historical incidence creating an unfair advantage: an infant industry case!

Price Discrimination

So far I have considered the case of deflection of production and investment where the price of imported raw materials is the same in both countries 1 and 2. Due to certain institutional factors, however, the price may be different for the two countries, even if they import from the same source, i.e. W practises price discrimination. In such circumstances the cost of imported raw materials and semi-manufactured goods will be different for the potential FTA partners, even though the quantity of these factors per unit of output is the same for both countries.

The price equations then become:

$$P_1 = q \cdot p_1^* + q^* \cdot p_{3,1}^* \, (1 + t_1^*) \tag{iii''}$$
$$P_2 = q \cdot p_2^* + q^* \cdot p_{3,2}^* \, (1 + t_2^*) \tag{iv''}$$

where $p_{3,1}^* \neq p_{3,2}^*$.

A new definition of comparative cost advantage is then necessary since the cost of both imported raw materials and domestic materials is different for the FTA potential partners. Hence, instead of $p_1^* < p_2^*$, comparative advantage must relate to:

$$q \cdot p_1^* + q^* \cdot p_{3,1}^* < q \cdot p_2^* + q^* \cdot p_{3,2}^* \tag{viii}$$

i.e. comparative advantage relates to the sum of both components of production, and rightly so.

Substituting (iii″) and (iv″) into condition (i) gives:

$$q \cdot p_2^* + q^* \cdot p_{3,2}^* (1 + t_2^*) < q \cdot p_1^* + q^* \cdot p_{3,2}^* (1 + t_1^*) \quad (\text{i}')$$

If deflection of production and investment were to take place, then the formation of the FTA must result in condition (i′) being satisfied. Rearranging (i′) gives:

$$q(p_2^* - p_1^*) < q^* [p_{3,1}^* (1 + t_1^*) - p_{3,2}^* (1 + t_2^*)] \qquad (\text{v}')$$

which is Balassa's proposition restated to take into account the different definition of comparative advantage.

This section of course relates to the case where both countries are producing the same commodity initially. The case where only one country is involved prior to the formation of the FTA does not require the price details: *deflection of production and investment is never possible under such circumstances.*

Moreover, one could consider more complicated situations, but the more complicated the situation, the less clear is Balassa's proposition.

Conclusion

In conclusion it must be emphasised that Balassa is referring to deflection of production and investment in terms of *shifts* in production, i.e. only one of the potential partners is producing the commodity initially. I have demonstrated that Balassa's proposition has no logical validity under such circumstances: *deflection of production and investment can occur only when both potential partners are producing the same commodity initially.* It must also be stressed, however, that this possibility is based on very strong assumptions, particularly the assumption that the country with the domestic cost advantage has a higher tariff rate of duty on imported intermediate goods. This suggests that the governments concerned are not only irrational in determining their tariff structures, but also display ignorance of the effective protection of trade impediments.

My analysis also suggests the conclusion that there are situations where countries should be advised to establish customs unions rather than free trade areas. This can be explained thus: the theory of economic integration states that a customs union or a free trade area is more likely to bring benefits if the potential partners are initially competitive but potentially complementary; deflection of production and investment (given the stated assumptions) is likely to occur only under the same circumstances; the formation of a customs union will eliminate the tariff differential and will therefore dispose of the possibility of deflection.

A Theory of Free Trade Areas

Shibata (1967) attempts an analysis which specifically incorporates the 'rules of origin' as part of the definition of a FTA:

> a free-trade area is defined . . . as an international grouping of . . . countries, each of which agrees to exempt from the tariffs and quantitative restrictions which it generally imposes on imported products, that part of those products which have originated or are produced in the territories of the other members of the group. (Shibata 1967, p. 68).

Shibata's analysis relates to two potential FTA partners, countries 1 and 2, and the outside world, W. He assumes the following:

(a) both countries 1 and 2 import an *identical product* from W;
(b) countries 1 and 2 also *produce wholly domestically perfect substitutes* for this commodity, call them domestic-substitutes for short;
(c) countries 1 and 2 impose different specific tariffs (which remain constant throughout the analysis) such that $t_1 > t_2$;
(d) the traditional trade theory assumptions: normal supply and demand curves for countries 1 and 2 and a perfectly

elastic W supply curve for this commodity; perfect competition in both the commodity and factor markets in all three countries; complete absence of transport costs; perfect factor mobility within each country, but complete lack of mobility across national frontiers; the only trade impediment is tariffs, which are defined as 'effective protective duties'; and fixed rates of exchange.

Given these assumptions, the domestic price of this product in the initial situation is equal to $P_W(1 + t_1)$ and $P_W(1 + t_2)$ in countries 1 and 2 respectively, where P_W is W's import supply price. When countries 1 and 2 form a FTA, the 'rules of origin' dictate that the domestic-substitute can be traded freely, while the identical import remains subject to tariffs. Shibata claims that this differential treatment of the identical product may create an 'artificial price differentiation' between the imported product and its identical domestic-substitute. He explains this as follows: since $t_1 > t_2$ then $P_W(1 + t_1) > P_W(1 + t_2)$, which means that the formation of the FTA will result in country 1 importing this product from its partner. This implies that the joint domestic-substitute supply curve for the two partners becomes the effective supply for country 1's market. Since both supply curves are normal (by assumption), the joint supply curve must also be upward sloping. If country 1's demand is sufficiently large, the FTA price of this product will rise above $P_W(1 + t_2)$ – country 2's price. When the FTA price for the domestic-substitute rises, consumers in country 2 will cease to purchase it since they can buy the identical import at the constant initial price $P_W(1 + t_2)$. However, this higher FTA domestic-substitute price will induce producers in country 2 to produce and sell their entire output to consumers in country 1. Hence the *identical product* will have two different prices depending on its area of origin.

Shibata then discusses the implications of this differential pricing. When country 1's domestic-substitute price falls because of the increased effective supply curve, country 1's producers will curtail their production (production effect) and its consumers will expand their consumption of this product (consumption effect). Moreover, since the new domestic-substitute price is higher than country 2's original price, the producers in that country will expand their production (production effect), but because there is no change in the price of the identical import there will be no consumption effect here. Given the specified assumptions, these production and consumption effects will result in certain changes in trade between the three countries, the extent of which depends on the level of demand in country 1. For instance, if the joint FTA supply produces the same price in country 1 as initially – $P_W(1 + t_1)$ – then country 1's producers will remain unaffected, but part of the imports that used to come from W into country 1 will then come via country 2, disguised in the form of domestic-substitutes produced there.

Shibata's analysis is conducted on the assumption of perfect competition and that the partners import an 'identical product' and produce 'domestically perfect substitutes' for this product. In spite of this, he finds it perfectly reasonable to mention that 'the differential treatment of the identical product according to its origin may create an artificial price differentiation between the area-origin product and the non-area origin product,' (Shibata 1967, p. 68) which of course directly contradicts the assumptions of perfect competition. How possible is it to identify products by source without differentiating, i.e. labelling, them? Once the product is differentiated, the assumption of a single demand curve becomes unacceptable. Hence, an analysis based on such premises should not be taken seriously.

Notes

1 One could argue that the effective price is that facing the government rather than the consumer, in which case both countries will import from the rest of the world. But if that were the case, the initial conditions would have to be stated accordingly. Needless to say, this would be a highly unorthodox procedure!

2 W.M. Corden (1972) coined the term 'made to measure tariffs'. The term is meant to indicate that protection is positively related to inefficiency, hence suggesting rational tariff imposing authorities.

3 These relate to the regulations introduced in free trade areas to ensure that member countries claim tariff exemptions only for

commodities originating within their territories – cf. European Free Trade Association 1960 and 1976.

4 The assumption that prices are cost determined is very unrealistic, to say the least. It is, however, a very necessary assumption at this stage and for reasons that will become apparent shortly.

5 The most general type of production function is the CES production function. It could take the form:

$$O_x = [AxK^{-nx} + axL^{-nx}]^{-1/nx}$$

where O_x is the value added in industry x deflated by the price of commodity x; L and K stand for labour and capital respectively (which, for our purposes, can stand for domestic and imported factors) and Ax, ax, nx are parameters.

The Stanford Group has proved that $1/(nx + 1) = zx$ is the elasticity of substitution between K and L in this industry. It is assumed to be constant.

Here it is assumed that nx is infinite so that zx is equal to zero. This reduces the production function to a Leontief fixed coefficients production function. cf. Minhas 1962 and Arrow, Chenery, Minhas and Solow 1961.

4

Orthodox Customs Union Theory: (1) Domestic Distortions and Scale Economies

A J JONES

In Chapter 2 it was shown that the traditional Vinerian analysis was unable to explain the formation of a customs union as a rational act of economic policy-making. In retrospect, however, such a conclusion is not too disturbing, given the recognition that it is an inevitable result of the assumptions, which are precisely those required to preclude the justification of the use of any form of tariff protection. By introducing less restrictive assumptions, modern tariff theory does now recognise a number of rational explanations for the use of non-discriminating tariffs, and it would seem that these models might also provide more suitable frameworks for the analysis of preferential tariff arrangements such as customs unions than does the free trade basis of Vinerian theory. In essence, two main sets of arguments for the use of non-discriminating tariffs can be identified: 'first best' arguments, which in the main rely on the ability of tariff policy to influence the terms of trade, and 'second best' arguments, which present a case for the use of tariffs where domestic distortions from conditions of Pareto optimality exist and where there are effective constraints on the choice of superior policy alternatives.

The Vinerian model in its basic form excludes the 'first best' arguments for tariffs by the 'small country' assumption of constant terms of trade in the foreign economies and, as traditionally presented, the model also implicitly excludes arguments based on the existence of domestic distortions. Attempts, however, have been made to extend the model in both directions and we shall consider the 'second best' arguments in the remainder of this chapter, whilst abstracting from the 'first best' by retaining the assumption of constant terms of trade in the rest of the world. This procedure will be reversed in the following chapter to enable us to examine the implications of the 'first best' arguments free from the complications raised by issues of the 'second best'.

Domestic Distortions in the Home Country

An underlying weakness in the Vinerian approach is that it simply overlooked the problem of considering the basis of policy choice by national governments. This is, in general, an area which economists have neglected but for our purposes it will suffice to use the naive but widely employed assumption that governments seek to maximise a social welfare function, given the constraints that might affect policy choice. If all policy instruments are regarded as costlessly and freely variable, it would follow that governments would always employ a policy of optimal intervention, the basic principles of which are (a) that only first best policy instruments should be used to intervene at the exact points in the economy at which distortions arise to prevent the market mechanism from producing the socially optimal result and (b) that such policy instruments should be set at the optimal rate in order to offset the distortion exactly and so produce the desired result.

Since we shall continue to abstract from problems of time, uncertainty and money, the analysis here need identify only five policy instruments. Lump-sum income transfers are the first best method for redistributing income and this assumption that these are being optimally used provides the basis for the derivation of the social indifference curves on which both demand functions and welfare judgements are based. Similarly, taxes (and subsidies) directed at factor use, at production and at consumption provide the first best means of offsetting the externalities and market imperfections which arise, respectively, in the factor market, in production and in consumption. It is the (implicit) assumption of the traditional model outlined in Chapter 2 that these are also being optimally employed which enables the demand and supply curve diagrams of that chapter to be used to convey information about social as well as private valuation of the costs and benefits of domestic production and consumption. As with the domestic policy instruments, it then follows that taxes (and subsidies) directed at international trade are also first best policy instruments whose optimal use arises when (and only when) they are used to offset externalities (such as 'public good' arguments for greater national self-sufficiency) and market imperfections (such as monopoly power) which occur in international trade.

Given this picture of unconstrained optimal policy choice, it follows that, as no such foreign distortions are postulated in the traditional model of customs union theory, the optimal tariff policy is one of free trade. Both the initial tariff and the policy of forming a customs union with the partner country are therefore not rational policy choices, and the inconclusive result of the attempt to rank them should occasion little surprise.

This result, however, rests upon the assumption that all first best policy instruments are freely and costlessly variable. If this assumption is abandoned, it is helpful to distinguish between constraints on domestic policies and constraints on trade policies. The latter will be considered subsequently but, initially, the argument will follow the attempts by Floystad (1975) and Yu and Scully (1976) to examine customs union theory whilst allowing for the existence of domestic distortions (including those arising from the existence of public goods) and the presence of constraints on the use of domestic policies. Throughout this chapter, these constraints will be exemplified by the assumption that production taxes and subsidies cannot be varied (because of domestic 'political' restraints), though, by analogy, the resulting analysis could be applied to the loss of any other domestic first best instrument.

The effect of this is to introduce the possibility that the social and private valuation of costs of domestic production may differ. This is illustrated in figure 4.1, which shows the

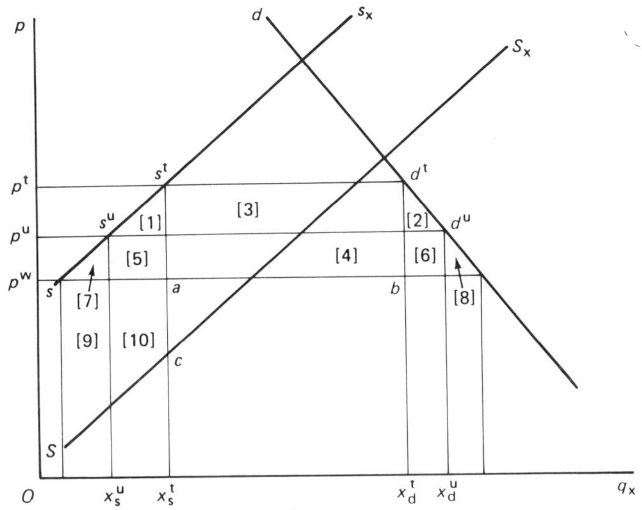

Figure 4.1 *Domestic Distortions in the Home Country*

same economy as figure 2.6 in Chapter 2 but with the introduction of the distinction between the socially valued marginal cost curve of the domestic production of importables, SS_x, and the privately valued marginal cost curve, ss_x, which, in the absence of any government action, would also be the domestic supply curve of commodity x. We shall not be concerned here with the source of the distinction, but it could arise because of external economies in the production of commodity x, which might originate in the public good argument that a collective preference exists for greater domestic production of importables. With no constraints on policy choice, optimal intervention would involve the use of a production subsidy which would shift ss_x to coincide with SS_x. Given the assumed constraint, however, the optimal use of tariff policy changes. Imposing a tariff still brings about consumption effect losses and privately valued production effect losses but it is now also necessary to take into account the difference between the social and the private valuation of marginal opportunity costs of production. Thus, in the case of the non-discriminatory tariff policy which raises the effective foreign supply curve of importables to the home market to $p^t d^t$, the consumption and privately valued production effects are shown by areas (2 + 6 + 8) and (1 + 5 + 7) respectively. The socially valued production effect, however, is the net gain shown by the area (9 + 10). In the case illustrated, this gain exceeds the consumption loss and, indeed, the diagram has been drawn so that this non-discriminatory tariff represents the (second best) optimal rate, such that the marginal consumption loss ($d^t b$) is just equal to the marginal production gain (ac).

As I have pointed out elsewhere, however, the introduction of constraints on domestic policy choice in the home country is insufficient to enable the small country model to provide a rational justification for the formation of a customs union (Jones 1980). A full consideration of this problem involves distinguishing between the optimal effective preferential tariff policy and the formation of a customs union. By introducing two foreign economies into the theory of tariffs, customs union theory identified two policy instruments for optimal intervention in international trade – taxes (and subsidies) on trade with the partner and taxes (and subsidies) on trade with the rest of the world. Given the 'small country' assumption of fixed foreign terms of trade, the effect of any non-discriminatory policy is for all trade to be with the lower cost source of supply – the rest of the world. To have any effect on the source of trade it is necessary for the home country to adopt an effective preferential policy, such that the rate of duty on imports from the partner is lower than on those from the rest of the world by at least the difference in the terms of trade of the two foreign sources of supply (i.e. by at least $p^w p^u$). If there are no constraints on policy choice, this preferential policy need not involve the formation of a customs union (or a free trade area). Thus, consider first the adoption of the minimal effective tariff preference to alter the pattern of trade. With a (specific) tariff duty of $p^w p^t$ on imports from the rest of the world, an effective preferential policy is achieved by imposing the (lower) tariff rate $p^u p^t$ on imports from the partner. The result of this is to leave the effective foreign supply curve of importables as $p^t d^t$ with domestic consumption and production as with the optimal non-discriminatory tariff. Given the preference, however, $p^{t}d^{t}$ is no longer solely the (tariff-inclusive) export supply curve of the rest of the world, but is also the (tariff-inclusive) export supply curve of the partner. Domestic consumers may therefore buy from either source and, to the extent that imports are diverted from the lower cost source of supply, the sole result of this for the home country is a reduction in tariff revenue. In the limit, if the tariff preference is just sufficient to divert all trade to the partner, the home country's tariff revenue loss is shown by area (4), i.e. it is equal to the Vinerian trade diversion effect. Compared to the optimal non-discriminatory policy, the granting of such a preference is thus an unambiguous source of loss to the home country. It is, however, superior to the form of preferential policy implied by membership of a customs union.

This can be seen by again introducing the alternative policy choice of the non-discriminatory reduction in the import tariff to the level (the 'A' rate) at which the domestic terms of trade would be identical to those which would result from membership of the customs union. As in Chapter 2, the 'A' tariff is shown in figure 4.1 as the specific rate $p^{w}p^{u}$. Comparison of this policy with that of joining the customs union again shows identical effects for the internal terms of trade, production, consumption, the volume of trade, and economic surplus. As before the sole difference between the two policies is that, with the non-preferential tariff policy, imports from the rest of the world yield tariff revenue measured by area (4 + 5 + 6) whereas, with the customs union, these imports are diverted to the tariff-free source, the partner. Unlike the case examined in the previous chapter, however, the net welfare effect of moving from the initial tariff to the 'A' rate is inevitably one of loss since the initial tariff is here assumed to be the (second best) optimal non-discriminatory tariff. Thus, compared to this optimal initial policy, the following welfare losses associated with different policy choices can be noted:

(a) the preferential lowering of the tariff on imports from the partner to the level $p^{u}p^{t}$, whilst retaining the tariff rate $p^w p^t$ on imports from the rest of the world, causes a maximum loss of tariff revenue equal to the Vinerian measure of trade diversion, i.e. area (4);

(b) the unilateral non-discriminatory tariff reduction from the optimal rate, $p^w p^t$, to the 'A' rate, $p^w p^u$, results in a consumption effect gain, area (2 + 6) which is outweighed by the (socially valued) production effect loss, area (10); and

(c) membership of the customs union (or free trade area) with the initial tariff retained on imports from the rest of the world, whilst the tariff on imports from the partner is completely removed, involves the Cooper and Massell measure of trade diversion loss, area (4 + 5 + 6) in addition to the loss identified for (b).

Thus, membership of the customs union appears unambiguously worse than either (a) or (b), with these also being inferior to the initial position (which itself remains only a second best choice, depending for its validity on the existence of constraints on the use of domestic policy instruments).

Unfortunately, both the papers of Floystad and Yu and Scully fail to reach such a conclusion because they pursue the traditional approach of starting from a purely arbitrary initial tariff position. This enables them to depict cases where the initial tariff choice is so inappropriate that, compared to it, even membership of the customs union brings net gain to the home country. Such an argument, however, could be used as a justification for membership of the customs union only if superior policy alternatives are not available. Since the superior policy alternatives include other forms of tariff policy it thus follows that whatever constraints exist on the use of domestic policy instruments, the justification of membership of a customs union within this framework must rest upon the existence of constraints on tariff policy. This issue too is ignored by Floystad and Yu and Scully, though, in fact, various constraints on the use of tariff policy do exist, both in the form of international treaty obligations and the fear of international retaliation if these are not complied with and, possibly, in the form of domestic political constraints.

Thus, it could well be argued that effective external constraints do prevent at least the members of GATT from pursuing preferential policies other than membership of a customs union or free trade area (since these are the only forms of preferential trading arrangements countenanced by GATT). Equally some external constraints do exist on the unilateral raising of non-discriminatory tariffs and such constraints could be used to explain why the initial tariff may be below the optimal rate. A simple adaptation of the earlier argument, however, shows that, starting from a sub-optimal position, the effects of membership of the customs union are still equivalent to the effects of a non-discriminatory reduction to the 'A' rate, plus the inevitable trade diversion loss of foregone tariff revenue associated with the 'A' rate. With the 'A' rate being below the (sub-optimal) initial rate, it follows that the first of these effects involves a move away from the optimum position and is also a source of loss so that the initial non-discriminatory tariff is superior to joining the customs union. The possibility of the initial tariff being inferior to the customs union thus depends on the initial tariff being above the optimal level since then the reduction to the 'A' rate may bring sufficient gain to outweigh the trade diversion loss. Indeed, the basic model outlined in Chapter 2 may be regarded as a special case of this result for with the optimal tariff being zero in that model any reduction from the initial (positive) import duty to the 'A' rate must involve net gain to set against trade diversion loss. With no external constraints on unilateral non-discriminatory tariff reductions, however, the obvious policy choice is then the non-preferential tariff reduction to the optimum rate, which is unambiguously superior to membership of the customs union. Thus, the only possible rationale for membership of a customs union in such circumstances must rest upon the existence of domestic constraints on non-preferential tariff reductions (which are not equally effective in preventing membership of a customs union).

Can the model be extended to provide a rationale for the existence of such constraints? Consider the following. The model outlined so far has relied on the (costless) maintenance of full employment and balance of payments equilibrium as producers reallocate resources from the production of importables to the production of exportables. Thus, returning to figure 2.3 we may recall that the price change from p' to p'' not only had effects on reducing production and increasing imports of x but did so whilst retaining full employment and balance of payments equilibrium by expanding production and exports of y. We must now recognise that, in a world of imperfect knowledge, specific factors and social costs of factor mobility, this argument ignores the costs and delays which might be associated with the expansion of the y-industry. Thus, consider the extreme case in which production and consumption of x respond immediately to the change in price without any immediate expansion in the y-industry. The drop in the y-value of the output of x shown by area (VII + V) and the increase in the volume of imports ($x''_s x'_s + x'_d x''_d$) are then likely to be associated with unemployment and the emergence of a balance of payments deficit. Given the obvious difficulties found in dealing with such problems, it is perhaps not surprising that there may be reluctance to face such adjustment costs even for the longer-term advantages of improved resource allocation. As we have already seen, however, both the adoption of the 'A' tariff and membership of a customs union involve exactly the same change in the internal terms of trade and require the same response from producers. Consequently, given the trade diversion loss which membership of the customs union involves, the rationale for preferring such a policy must lie in the judgement that producers in the y-industry must respond more rapidly to the same change in the terms of trade when it is produced by joining a customs union than when it results from a unilateral non-preferential tariff reduction. In a world of perfect knowledge, it would be difficult to explain such a differential response. But arguably, in a world of imperfect knowledge, the perception of the advantages of expanding production (and exports) of y may occur more rapidly when it results from membership of the customs union than when it is due to unilateral tariff reductions by the country concerned. This is because membership of a customs union will also involve the elimination of the partner's tariff on imports of y from the home country and the possibility that this act may serve as a clearer stimulus to the advantages of expanding the y-industry in the home country than the internal terms of trade changes caused by a tariff-cutting policy. If this were the case, the adjustment costs associated with lagged responses to changes in relative prices may be smaller and last for a shorter time as a result of joining a customs union rather than adopting a non-preferential tariff reduction. In such circumstances (especially given the short-run focus of many political decisions), a rationale for joining a customs union can be provided if:

(a) the (Vinerian) trade creation gain exceeds the (Vinerian) trade diversion loss, plus the adjustment costs associated with membership of the customs union, so that such a policy is superior to the initial tariff;
(b) the country is prevented by external constraints from pursuing potentially superior preferential trading arrangements; and
(c) adjustment costs associated with unilateral tariff-cutting policies are great enough to outweigh the greater resource reallocation benefits that they would bring.

In addition, a 'non-economic' rationale for membership of a customs union can be introduced at this stage. Although first best economic arguments for the use of tariffs rely largely on variable terms of trade, first best 'non-economic' arguments can also be introduced by postulating the existence of public goods associated with international trade. Thus greater national self-sufficiency, if seen as a public good, provides a first best argument for the use of non-discriminatory tariffs. Similarly, if it is postulated that there is a collective preference for trade with the partner (political 'friend') as opposed to trade with the rest of the world (political 'rival'/'enemy'), then preferential trade taxes and subsidies are the first best policy choice. Thus, given the existence of external constraints on such forms of discriminatory policies, membership of a customs union may prove to be a superior second best alternative to any non-discriminatory tariff. Indeed the original formation of the EEC may be partly explained in these terms, with the public good benefits of greater intra-European trade being viewed as the reduction in the risk of future wars between France and Germany and possibly with a collective preference for the reduction of imports from the USA in the period of 'the dollar shortage'.

Such an example, however, goes beyond the confines of the 'small country' model, since both France and Western Germany (and other countries) can be viewed as potential beneficiaries from this effect, and points to a further crucial weakness in the traditional model: by concentrating attention solely on the home country, the analysis excludes the effects that the home country's policy decisions may have on the partner and the rest of the world.

The 'Small Union' Model

To rectify this weakness, it is helpful to proceed by retaining the assumption that the terms of trade of the rest of the world are fixed, whilst recognising the existence of the partner as another 'small' economy which can be modelled in the same way as the home economy. The importance of considering both the partner and the home country has been stressed by Massell (1968) but, except for a well-known article by Johnson (1965a), only Dutta (1968–9) seems to have examined the domestic distortions/public good arguments within the framework of customs union theory. Unlike Johnson's argument, which examines customs union formation only as a by-product of a more general argument, Dutta's article provides a comprehensive treatment of the issues within the framework of the three-country two-commodity general equilibrium model. Unfortunately though, despite an ingenious but complicated use of the geometrical tools of two-commodity space, most of Dutta's argument is forced to abstract from the issues of substitution in consumption. Further, it concentrates on the comparison of membership of a customs union with a policy of free trade rather than addressing itself to the question of whether or not a rationale exists for joining a customs union when alternative tariff policy choices are available. As shown elsewhere (Jones 1979), however, this question can be tackled relatively simply by an extension of the methods of general equilibrium demand and supply curve analysis so far outlined.

A special case of this extended model is illustrated in figure 4.2. In part (a) of the diagram, dd_x, ss_x and SS_x have the same interpretation as in earlier diagrams, thus suggesting that some external economy/public good is associated with production of commodity x in the home country. The partner economy is represented by similar functions in part (b) of the diagram where identical notation is used except for the superscript * to distinguish the partner's from the home economy's functions. Thus, the partner is also represented as having an external economy/public good linked to production of x. As p^w is again the constant terms of trade of the rest of the world, a policy of free trade would result in both economies being importers of commodity x from the rest of the world if they failed to take domestic action to offset the distortion arising from the external economy. By accepting the existence of restraints in both economies on the use of first best domestic policy instruments, the non-discriminatory

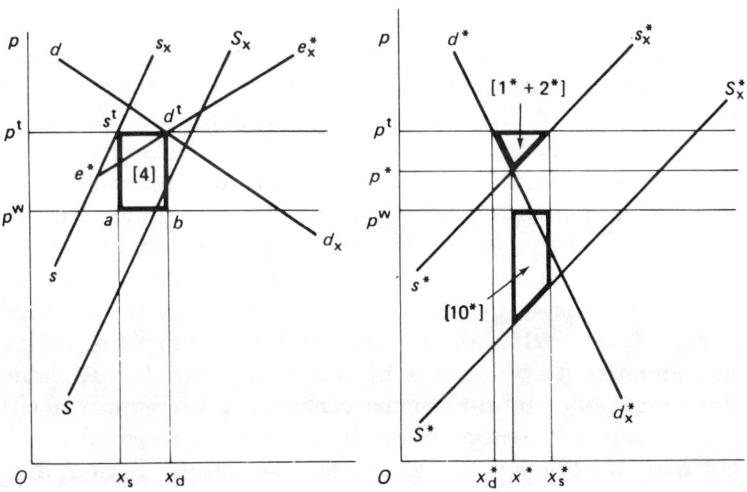

(a) *The Home Economy*

(b) *The Partner Economy*

Figure 4.2 *The 'Small Union' Model*

use of import tariffs can bring (socially valued) welfare gains to both economies. In the simple example shown in figure 4.2, the (second best) optimal trade policy for both economies is that which raises the internal terms of trade to p^t. For the home country, this can be achieved solely by the use of the non-preferential import tariff, $p^w p^t$, as a result of which domestic production will be x_s, consumption x_d, and imports from the rest of the world ($x_s x_d$) produce the tariff revenue shown by $as^t d^t b$, i.e. area (4). For the partner, however, although the optimal trade policy also includes a non-preferential import tariff of $p^w p^t$, it additionally requires that this should be combined with the same rate of export subsidy for, at the internal terms of trade shown by p^t, there would be domestic excess supply of commodity x in the partner, which could be sustained only by exporting the excess ($x_d^* x_s^*$) at the price (p^w) dictated by the terms of trade of the rest of the world.

If both countries could costlessly adopt such optimal non-discriminatory trade policies, there would be no basis for preferential action by either country. In addition to the constraints on the choice of trade policy considered earlier in this chapter, however, this case suggests a further external constraint on the use of optimal non-discriminatory trade policies as the use of export subsidies runs counter to the provisions of GATT. Accordingly, even if the partner sets its import tariff at $p^w p^t$, without the use of export subsidies the net outcome for the partner would be for its economy to settle at the self-sufficiency position with internal terms of trade p^*. Whilst this is superior to free trade or to any position of limited imports of commodity x, it is inferior to a policy that would enable the partner to export x. With the assumed constraints on the use of the first best domestic policy instruments and on the use of export subsidies, no available unilateral policy by the partner can achieve any improvement on this self-sufficiency policy. It can gain, however, if it can persuade the home country to enter into a preferential trading agreement which allows the partner to export commodity x to the home market.

In figure 4.2, the export supply curve of the partner, $e^* e_x^*$, has been obtained from its domestic demand and supply curves in the same manner as outlined for the home country in Chapter 2. It is shown in part (a) of the diagram as an addition to the domestic supply curve of the home country to give the joint union supply curve to the home market, se^*d^t. Such a supply curve becomes operative if the home country removes its initial tariff on trade with the partner, whilst retaining it on imports from the rest of the world. In general the optimal preferential policy from the joint viewpoint of the home and partner economies is determined where the marginal net gains (which accrue to the partner) are equal to the marginal net losses (which are suffered by the home country). In the special case illustrated in figure 4.2, such an optimal preferential policy is equivalent to forming a customs union with common external tariff $p^w p^t$ but, although this is generally not the case (i.e. other preferential trading arrangements will usually be superior to a customs union), given the external constraints on alternative forms of preferential policy, this simplification has the value of identifying the crucial comparison between the optimal available unilateral policy and the optimal available preferential arrangement. From the home country's viewpoint in the example shown, there is no effect on its internal terms of trade (which remain at p^t), on production, consumption, the volume of trade or economic surplus (whether privately or socially valued). The one change that does occur is the diversion of imports from the rest of the world to the partner, as a result of which the home country suffers the trade diversion loss of tariff revenue shown by area (4). If the joint union supply curve had cut the price line p^t to the left of d^t, the sole difference from the case shown would have been a diminished trade diversion loss as some trade would have been retained with the rest of the world. On the other hand, if $e^*e^*_x$ had intersected dd_x below d^t, membership of the customs union would not only incorporate the trade diversion loss but would also involve changes in the terms of trade, production and consumption for the home country and therefore the further net losses associated with the move from the optimum to the 'A' tariff rate, as identified in the small country model discussed earlier in this chapter.

Thus, as with the basic model, it appears that the home

country unambiguously loses when membership of a customs union is compared to the optimal unilateral trade policy. In the 'small union' framework, however, unlike the earlier argument, it is also necessary to examine the changes that occur in the partner. Starting from the initial position of self-sufficiency, the partner earns no tariff revenue either before or after union. The result of membership of the union, however, is to allow the partner's terms of trade to rise to p^t with the consequent changes in production and consumption as exports of x become $x_s^*x_d^*$. As a result, the partner benefits from the privately valued gains from specialisation and exchange shown by area (1* + 2*) and in addition obtains the further socially valued gain due to the external economy/public good associated with increased production of commodity x in the partner and shown in figure 4.2 by area (10*). These unambiguous gains to the partner can outweigh the losses to the home country (as they do in figure 4.2). From the viewpoint of the union as a whole, therefore, the joint policy of forming the customs union can be superior to the best available unilateral policies, though, from the viewpoint of the home country alone, the attractiveness of such joint action would presumably depend on arrangements for a satisfactory *quid pro quo* to offset the loss that it would otherwise suffer.

Again, it is tempting to apply this analysis to the development of economic integration in Western Europe, and in particular to the controversy over UK membership. Thus, suppose that commodity x in figure 4.2 is regarded as agricultural products, with the UK being the home country and the rest of the EEC being the partner economy. The model in figure 4.2 then points to the unambiguous trade diversion loss to the UK that is a widely accepted result of acceptance of the Common Agricultural Policy (CAP) and, thus, to the need to identify alternative sources of gain arising from other aspects of UK membership of the EEC (especially as the UK's actual loss due to acceptance of the CAP is likely to be greater than the trade diversion loss alone, both because the UK's domestic agricultural policy had proved more able to use theoretically superior policy instruments and because the actual CAP seems far from optimal even on second best grounds – see El-Agraa 1980, Chapter 7).

Economies of Scale in the Small Union Model

One of the most widely canvassed sources of such gains for the UK from membership of the EEC rests upon the existence of economies of scale rather than the constant or increasing costs postulated so far. Although Cooper and Massell (1965b) and Mead (1968) introduced both economies of scale and public good arguments into an examination of customs union formation for less developed countries, surprisingly little rigorous attention has been given to this problem. The exception to this is an article by Corden (1972), whose analysis, although it omits explicit consideration of public good arguments, does provide the basic framework with which we can approach the problem.

Instead of the (privately valued) marginal cost curves of earlier diagrams, it is helpful to represent the cost relationships in the two economies in terms of the average opportunity costs of producing commodity x, shown by AC_x for the home country and AC^*_x for the partner in figure 4.3. To

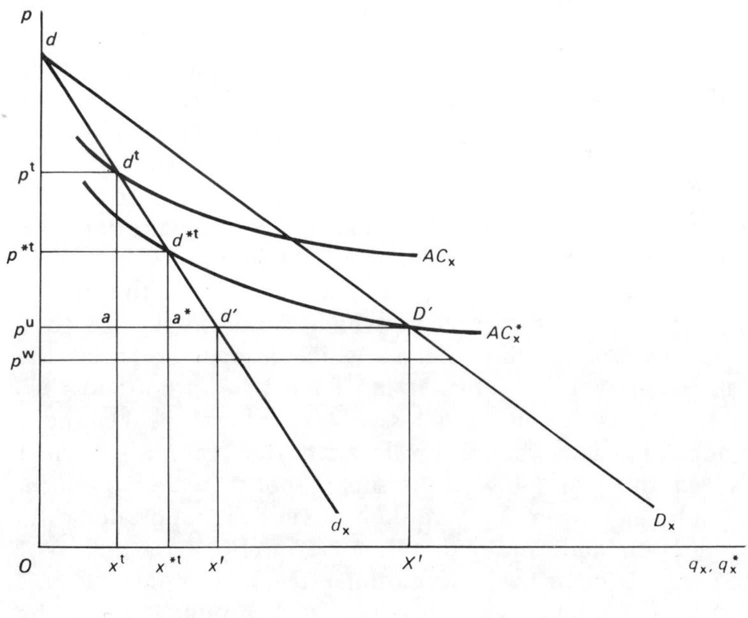

Figure 4.3 *Economics of Scale in the Small Union Model*

keep the diagram as simple as possible, the domestic demand curves for x (dd_x) are shown as being the same for both economies whilst dD_x represents the combined demand curve after the union is formed. The given terms of trade of the rest of the world are again shown by p^W and it is assumed that, whatever the scale of production, neither the home nor the partner industry can produce with (privately valued) average costs at or below this level (since, if average costs did fall below the terms of the trade of the rest of the world, production and exports of x could be achieved without protection).

As with the previous model, unless the presence of an uncorrected distortion between private and social costs is introduced, the optimal policy for both countries is free trade, with no internal production of x and no rationale for customs union formation. The introduction of an external economy/public good associated with the domestic production of x, however, plus the assumed unavailability of first best domestic policy means for dealing with this can produce a second best justification for the unilateral use of non-discriminatory tariffs and the superiority to this of joint preferential action. With the incorporation of falling costs into the model, the identification of the second best optimum tariff is different from the earlier cases and can be identified without having to show the socially valued cost curves in the diagram. This is because there is now only one possible rate which can be a candidate for the optimum tariff. This is the 'made-to-measure' tariff, which is defined as the rate of duty which just enables domestic production to supply the domestic market without the opportunity to obtain monopoly profits. It is therefore the rate which is required to raise the foreign supply price to the level at which domestic average costs equal average revenue (i.e. at which average costs cut the demand curve). Any higher tariff must be inferior to this, since it must result in a loss of consumers' surplus and a reduced (socially valued) production effect gain, which must exceed the monopoly profit such a policy would produce. Equally, any lower tariff would be unable to support domestic production and would therefore be inferior to a policy of free trade because the consumption effect loss would outweigh the tariff revenue associated with such a policy. Thus, the justification of the made-to-measure tariff as the second best optimal rate requires only the proof that it is superior to free trade. Compared to this policy any tariff, by raising prices, causes a consumption effect loss and since, by definition, the made-to-measure tariff gives the whole domestic market to the local producer there is no offsetting change in tariff revenue. Thus, the only potential source of gain to offset the consumption effect loss is due to the socially valued benefits associated with domestic production. Providing these production effect gains outweigh the consumption effect loss, the made-to-measure tariff is superior to free trade and is the second best unilateral trade policy. In principle, the socially valued production effect gain is shown by the volume of production multiplied by the amount by which socially valued average costs fall below the world price level. But, to simplify the diagram, this information is not shown in figure 4.3 though, to justify the initial made-to-measure tariff policies, it will be assumed that such socially valued production effect gains do exist for both the home and the partner economy. That being the case, the optimal unilateral trade policy of the home country is to impose the tariff rate $p^w p^t$, with domestic production and consumption of x being x^t. Similarly, the partner imposes the tariff $p^w p^{*t}$ and both produces and consumes x^{*t}. The superiority of joint action in forming a customs union then comes partly from the less inefficient of the local producers being able to take over the whole market and partly because, acting as a customs union, the two members can adopt a lower tariff as the made-to-measure rate for the common external tariff. In figure 4.3, this rate is shown as $p^w p^u$. By forming the union with such an external tariff, the partner increases production from x^{*t} to X' (thus increasing the socially valued production benefit) and increases consumption from x^{*t} to x'. The (privately valued) welfare change associated with this can be split into two components:

(i) the 'cost reduction' effect, $p^u p^{*t} d^{*t} a^*$, due to the reduced cost of supplying the initial level of domestic demand for x and
(ii) the 'pure' consumption effect, $a^* d^{*t} d'$, due to the response of consumers to the change in relative prices.

Both these components represent sources of welfare gain, so that the partner unambiguously gains from the formation of the union. The home country also benefits from the same kinds of privately valued welfare changes as the result of the fall in its internal terms of trade from p^t to p^u and the resulting expansion in consumption from x^t to x'. For the home country these gains are associated with the increased volume of trade (since imports of x grow from nothing to x') and can be thought of as providing an enhanced 'trade creation' effect. The distinction between the 'cost reduction' effect ($p^u p^t d^t a$) and the 'pure' consumption effect, ($ad^t d'$), however, is still a useful one to make, for the 'cost reduction' effect suggests the potential empirical significance of introducing economies of scale into the analysis. This is because, as all empirical investigations have shown, the welfare gains associated with the trade creation effects of the traditional model are small (see El-Agraa 1980, Chapter 5). In principle at least, however, the 'cost reduction' effect could be much larger. In the traditional model the trade creation gains are equal to *half of the increase in the volume of imports* multiplied by the fall in the internal terms of trade. The welfare gain from the cost reduction effect on the other hand, is equal to the potentially far greater *total volume of domestic demand* multiplied by the fall in the internal terms of trade. Nonetheless, whatever the size of the cost reduction effect, the home country will suffer a net loss from membership of the customs union (prior to receipt of any compensation from the partner) due to the loss of the public good benefits associated with domestic production of x. This follows because this production effect loss, by assumption of the superiority of the made-to-measure tariff to free trade, must be larger than the consumption effect yielded by comparison of those two policies, which, in turn, is clearly larger than the privately valued welfare effect shown above for the comparison of the made-to-measure tariff and membership of the customs union.

Although the home country loses, however, the union as a whole can obtain net gain because, in addition to the consumption effect gains in the partner, there are also the public good gains from the increased volume of production in the partner. Thus, provided an adequate *quid pro quo* can be arranged for the home country, the formation of a customs union in the presence of economies of scale, domestic distortions and constraints on the use of first best policy instruments can be justified as being superior to alternative trade policies. Similar results can be obtained where initial production of x is in either one or neither of the member countries, despite the fact that, in such cases, there may also be losses associated with trade diversion and trade suppression effects – see Corden 1972.

This conclusion is reinforced if the economies of scale are interpreted as economies accruing to an integrated industry rather than being plant economies of scale or economies of scale internal to a national industry. This is because the possibility then exists that, although one member's industry may gain control of the whole union market, the location of some of its producing units may be in the home country. Thus, unless the public good benefits of production are necessarily linked with domestic ownership of the industry, it may be that the production effects for the home economy may be less adverse than suggested in the previous argument, thereby suggesting the possibility of the outcome of joining the union being one of net gain in the home as well as the partner economy, even without the arrangement of a *quid pro quo*. Nonetheless, in the context of UK membership of the EEC, one is left with the hope that it is the UK which most closely approximates the role of the more competitive partner economy, though the empirical support for such a hope seems sadly lacking.

Of course, it might appear even more relevant to point out that the only basis for these gains is the assumed constraint on domestic policies (as well as on trade taxes) and that it would be much better for all economies if sufficient political will were applied to the problem of removing the constraints on domestic policy choice. The economies of scale argument, however, does suggest a potentially more powerful case for economic integration. In the argument up to this point, externalities and market imperfections, other than those which arise directly in international trade, have been regarded as confined to being within each country. If this assumption is relaxed, the possibility exists of private decisions taken in one country having external effects not only within that economy but for other countries as well. From a wider, international viewpoint even the optimal *national* use of first best policies may then be sub-optimal. In such a case the first best solution requires the establishment of international authorities with the power to use appropriate first best policies. The optimal limits of the jurisdiction of such international authorities are determined in principle by the equality of the marginal benefits from 'internalising' such externalities and the marginal costs associated with setting up (and controlling) such international authorities. Of course, in many cases such costs may be very high, especially in a changing world in which optimal policy intervention will require the capacity for flexible response, and the scope for the delegation of first best domestic policies to such international authorities has so far proved to be very limited. With international constraints on the use of tariff policies being more readily accepted, however, with the imperfect use of national policies to offset externalities and market imperfections which overflow national boundaries, and with such externalities being more significant among countries with close economic ties, it follows that a second best case may exist for the formation of a customs union between closely linked economies. Such a case is analogous to the second best case for the national use of tariffs in the presence of domestic distortions. Given the inability of the partners to adopt appropriate first best policies to offset distortions which are internal to the union, the optimal use of a second best instrument, such as the common external tariff, is justified.

5

Orthodox Customs Union Theory: (2) The Large Union Case

A J JONES

Since preferential policies always involve the trade diversion loss of tariff revenue which could have been obtained by the appropriate use of non discriminatory tariffs, the single country focus of traditional union theory is a poor guide to the rationale of customs union formation. By changing the focus of the analysis to examine the combined effects of membership of a customs union for both the home and the partner economy, rational 'second best' justifications for creating customs unions can be identified, but only in cases where there are assumed to be effective constraints on the use of superior domestic policy instruments and of certain forms of trade policy. By assuming constant terms of trade in the rest of the world, however, the analysis has so far excluded the traditional first best argument for tariffs – the optimum tariff argument for exploiting monopoly/monopsony power in international trade. To see how the introduction of this possibility affects the analysis of the formation of a customs union, it is helpful to exclude the second best arguments in the previous chapter by assuming that all domestic distortions are directly offset by appropriate use of first best domestic policy instruments and to regard each separate economy in the customs union model as being appropriately depicted by the same kind of domestic demand and supply curve diagrams as employed in Chapter 2 for the home country alone. As shown in that chapter (compare figures 2.3 and 2.5), it is then possible to derive import demand/export supply diagrams which can be used to examine the effects of the formation of a customs union. Such diagrams are particularly useful when, as here, it is necessary to examine the trade and welfare effects for three separate economies simultaneously.

Elsewhere the formulation of customs union theory has been identified as the 'large union' case to distinguish it both from the (traditional) 'small country' and 'small union' models previously considered (Jones 1979). This formulation has been the subject of a number of important contributions to the literature, perhaps most notably Arndt (1968 and 1969), Kemp (1969), Melvin (1969) and Takayama (1972), but, although these have avoided many of the pitfalls of the traditional approach, in varying degrees they have all fallen short of providing a full interpretation of the case in the context of optimal intervention analysis. It is this which is attempted here, rather than a critical review of any particular contributions (which, it may be noted however, rely extensively on the use of trade offer curves, i.e. on the two-commodity geometrical space counterparts of the trade demand and supply curves employed here).

The model is set out in figure 5.1, in which the basic functional relationships depicted are the import demand function for the home country, mm_x in part (a), and the export supply functions of the partner and the rest of the world, $e^*e^*_x$ and $e^w e^w_x$, respectively, in parts (b) and (c). From this basic information, it is then possible to derive the total foreign (tariff-free) export supply function facing the home country by adding $e^*e^*_x$ and $e^w e^w_x$ to obtain EE_x in part (a). Thus, for example, at terms of trade $p_0 = p^w_0$ the total quantity of commodity x supplied to the home market by foreign suppliers, x^t, is equal to x^{*t} exported from the partner, plus x^{wt} exported from the rest of the world. Equally, by combining the import demand function of the home country and the export supply function of the partner, it is possible to derive the net import demand curve, uu_x in part (c), of the customs union after its formation. Thus, for example, at terms of trade p^u, the net import demand of the union, x^{wu}, is equal to the total import demand of the home country, x^u, less the export supply of the partner, x^{*u}.

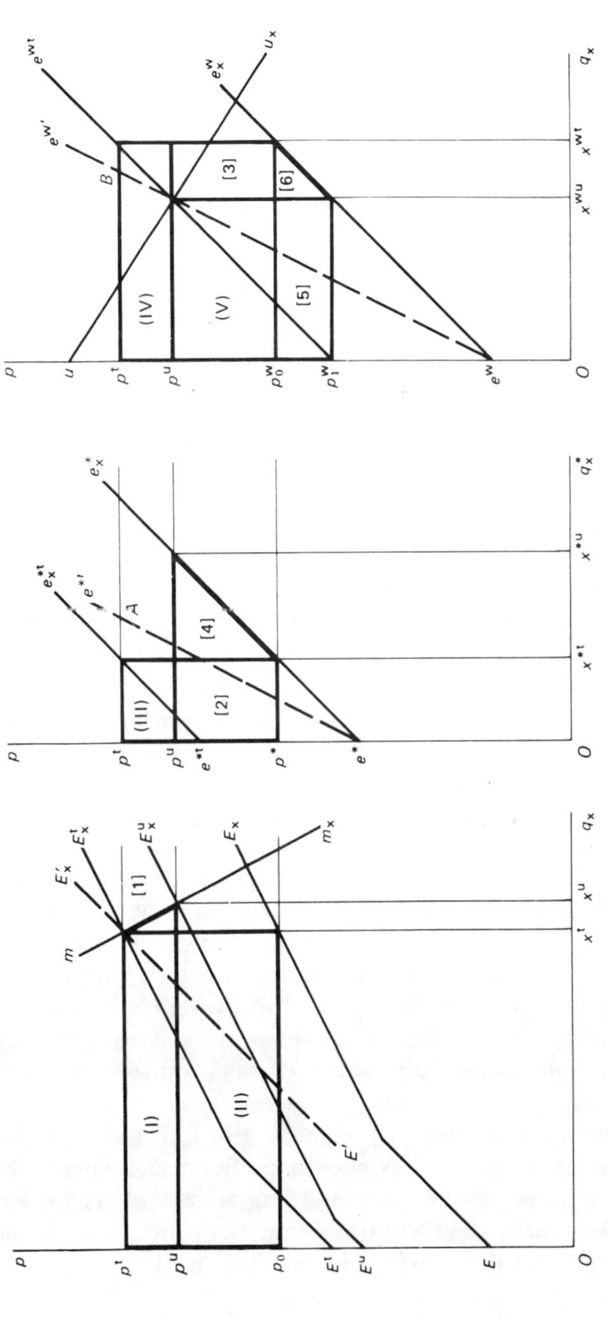

(a) *Trade of the Home Country*

(b) *Trade of the Partner*

(c) *Trade of the Rest of the World and the Customs Union*

Figure 5.1

From the home country's viewpoint, the various foreign export supply functions may be more helpfully regarded in their inverse form as showing the average cost to the home country of obtaining imports, so that, for example, $e^*e^*_x$ can also be identified as the average cost function for the home country of importing x from the partner. It then follows that it is possible to identify the corresponding marginal cost of importing functions. These are shown by the broken lines, $E'E'_x$, $e^*e^{*\prime}$, and $e^w e^{w\prime}$, which share the same intercept but have twice the slope of the average cost curves from which they are derived. Thus $e^*e^{*\prime}$ shows the marginal cost to the home country of importing x from the partner whilst $E'E'_x$ shows the marginal cost of importing from any source. Similarly $e^w e^{w\prime}$ shows the marginal cost of importing x from the rest of the world, both from the viewpoint of the home country alone and from the viewpoint of the combined membership of the customs union.

In addition to the functions so far identified in figure 5.1, it is also possible to show the impact of different trade policies by constructing the appropriate tariff-inclusive trade curves. Two major policy alternatives are illustrated. In one case the home country is shown as imposing a uniform specific import tariff of p_0p^t, thereby raising the tariff-inclusive import supply curves to the home market to $e^{*t}e^{*t}_x$ for trade with the partner, to $p^w_1e^{wt}$ for trade with the rest of the world and, by combining these, to $E^tE^t_x$ for imports from the whole world. The second case shown consists of a customs union in which the home country removes its tariff on imports from the partner whilst the same specific tariff as in the first case (p_0p^t) is adopted as the common external tariff of the union. In this case, the total import supply curve to the home market is shown by $E^uE^u_x$, which is obtained by adding the tariff-free supply curve of the partner ($e^*e^*_x$) to the tariff-inclusive supply curve of the rest of the world ($p^w_1e^{wt}$).

In essence the problem of optimal choice of trading policy for the separate economies shown in figure 5.1 falls within the general areas of oligopoly and bargaining theory because each participant is shown as possessing the power to influence the international terms of trade and because the outcome of any unilateral action will depend on the reaction to it by the other two economies. Accordingly, the analysis can proceed only by introducing assumptions about the determination of trade policies by the partner and the rest of the world and, in particular, about their reaction to policy changes of the home country.

Let us assume initially that both the partner and the rest of the world are unable to react in any way to the home country's choice of trade policy. The optimal policy of the home country can then be identified as being equivalent to the action of a profit-maximising, discriminating monopsonist. In general, the first order conditions for optimising behaviour require that marginal costs are equated with marginal benefits. In the example shown, the marginal costs of importing for the home country are shown by $E'E'_x$, whilst the marginal value of importing is shown by the import demand curve mm_x. Thus, the optimal volume of imports is shown as x^t and, as illustrated, this can be achieved by the imposition of the uniform specific tax p_0p^t on all imports. Discriminatory tariff policies, however, would produce a superior result with the optimal discriminatory policy requiring the marginal cost of importing from each separate source being equated with the marginal value of imports. This would be achieved by imposing a lower tariff on imports from the partner and a higher tariff on imports from the rest of the world, so that their tariff-inclusive export supply curves passed through points A and B respectively.

Given the likely external constraints on trade policies discussed in Chapter 4, however, it seems improbable that the home country could adopt such discriminatory policies without retaliation. Let us now, therefore, assume that the rest of the world will not react either to non-discriminatory tariffs or to the formation of a customs union, but will retaliate if alternative trade policies are adopted. From the home country's viewpoint, therefore, the optimum available unilateral trade policy is that shown by the non-discriminatory tariff p_0p^t and the adoption of this policy leads to imports of x^{*t} from the partner and x^{wt} from the rest of the world. It can be noticed that, if expressed in *ad valorem* terms, this tariff rate, p_0p^t/p_0, is equal to the inverse of the elasticity of the import supply function, EE_x, at the volume of imports x^t, which is, of course, a well-known formula for the optimum tariff.

Now let us further suppose that the partner is prepared to pursue a more active policy-making rôle than the rest of the world and is prepared to react to the home country's trade policy. One option available to it would be to retaliate by imposing its own optimum tariff on imports of y from the home country. Such a reaction would inevitably leave the home country worse off than with its initial, non-opposed, optimum policy and may possibly leave both countries worse off than if they had both retained free trade policies. As El-Agraa has pointed out elsewhere (1979), however, co-operation in tariff policies can be more attractive than retaliation. This is certainly the case here, for, with the rest of the world assumed to react neither to non-discriminatory tariffs nor to the formation of the customs union, the optimal policy from the joint viewpoint of the home country and the partner is to form a customs union with no barriers to intra-union trade and with a common external tariff set at the optimal rate determined by the elasticity of the union's import supply curve from the rest of the world. It must now be noted that figure 5.1 has been drawn so as to represent a particularly simple case of such a policy, because the optimum common external tariff is revealed as being identical to the initial unilateral optimum tariff of the home country. This is because, for the union, the marginal cost of importing from the rest of the world is shown by $e^w e^{w\prime}$, whilst the marginal value of imports is shown by the union import demand curve uu_x. Thus, x^{wu} is the optimum volume of union imports from the rest of the world, which will result from the imposition of the specific external tariff $e^w p_1^w = p_1^w p^u = p_0^w p^t$. This tariff can thus be identified as the optimum external tariff for the customs union and, just like the optimal level of a national tariff, it is simply related to the value of the elasticity of the appropriate import supply curve at the relevant point, i.e. (x^{wu}, p_1^w) on the rest of the world's export supply curve, $e^w e_x^w$ – see Takayama (1972), Chapter 16, for a formal proof. Thus, the effects of the policy change from the optimum unilateral tariff to membership of a customs union with the optimum external tariff are shown by comparison of the two policy alternatives depicted in figure 5.1. Initially, the home country has the domestic terms of trade p^{t} and is importing x^{t}, with x^{*t} of this being supplied by the partner and x^{wt} by the rest of the world. The corresponding domestic terms of trade for the partner and the rest of the world are shown as p^{*} and p^{w}_{0} respectively. After formation of the union, the terms of trade for the home country fall to p^{u}, with the total volume of imports increasing from x^{t} to x^{u} as the increase in trade with the partner (from x^{*t} to x^{*u}) outweighs the decrease in trade with the rest of the world (from x^{wt} to x^{wu}). Recalling the earlier terminology, it is appropriate to identify $x^{t}x^{u}$ as the volume of trade creation for the home country, $x^{*t}x^{*u}$ as the volume of trade creation for the partner, and $x^{wu}x^{wt}$ as the volume of trade diversion from the viewpoint of both the home country and the rest of the world. As a result of the changes in the domestic terms of trade, the following changes in economic surplus can then be identified:

(i) The home country benefits from an increase in economic surplus due to the fall in the price of its imports. This gain consists of two parts, that shown by area (I) being the terms of trade gain on existing imports and that shown by area (1) incorporating both the production and the consumption components of the trade creation effect for the home country;

(ii) The partner also receives an increase in economic surplus due to the increase in the price of its export good. This gain can also be divided into two parts, area (2) being the terms of trade effect on existing exports and area (4) being the trade creation effect for the partner;

(iii) The rest of the world, on the other hand, suffers a loss of economic surplus as a result of the fall in price of its exports. Again, this change can be divided into two parts, area (5) being the terms of trade effect for the remaining volume of its export and area (6) being the rest of the world's trade diversion effect.

In addition to these changes in economic surplus, the

welfare of the home country and, possibly, the partner is also affected by changes in tariff revenue. Initially, the tariff receipts of the home country are shown by area (I + II) whilst post-union tariff revenue is shown by area (V + 5). By the method of construction of the diagrams it follows that area (II) = area (2 + V + 3), so that, from the overall union viewpoint, the change in tariff receipts, i.e. area (V + 5) minus area (I + II) is equal to area (5 – 2 – 3 – I). If post-union tariff receipts are retained entirely by the home country, the net welfare effect for the home country of combining the change in economic surplus and tariff revenue is shown by area (1 + 5 – 2 – 3). Of the four components of this welfare effect, area (1) has already been identified as the trade creation effect for the home country, whilst areas (5) and (2) are simply the obverse of the terms of trade effects for the rest of the world and the partner, respectively. This leaves us with area (3), which is the traditional trade diversion effect for the home country.

Of course if, as is probable, post-union tariff receipts are paid into a central budget and are not entirely redistributed to the home country, the net welfare effect for the home country would be worse than this. Equally, the net welfare effect for the partner would be correspondingly better as its share of the tariff receipts would add to its unambiguous gain in economic surplus. From the combined viewpoint of the partner and the home country, both what happens to tariff receipts and the terms of trade effect on the partner's initial exports to the home country are solely concerned with the internal distribution of welfare. The net change in welfare for the union as a whole is thus equal to area (1 + 4 + 5 – 3), with the terms of trade gain *vis-à-vis* the rest of the world combining with the trade creation effects to outweigh the loss associated with trade diversion.

For the rest of the world, on the other hand, the effect of the formation of the customs union is one of unambiguous welfare loss due to the fall in its economic surplus, whilst, from the global viewpoint, the terms of trade effect on the rest of the world's exports to the union is purely distributional. Accordingly, the global welfare effect of the change in policy is equal to area (1 + 4 – 3 – 6), which may have either a positive or a negative value. It is, therefore, uncertain whether the replacement of the optimum tariff of the home country by the formation of a customs union will bring net welfare gain or loss. The result, however, does vindicate the empirical interest in identifying the volumes of trade creation and trade diversion as, from the global viewpoint, the sole sources of gain are trade creation effects and the sole sources of loss are associated with trade diversion.

Trade policies, however, are determined by national statesmen rather than any global authority and, with the rest of the world assumed to be unable to react to the loss inflicted on it by the formation of the customs union (which may well be a realistic assumption reflecting the diverse nature of the third economy that its naming implies), the issue of whether the customs union will be formed or not will depend on the effects for the member countries. The partner clearly gains compared with the unopposed optimum policy of the home country, but the net effect for the home country is uncertain and could well be negative, especially if it has to forego some of the post-union tariff revenue. It must be remembered, however, that (a) the partner could, in principle, compensate the home country because, with an optimal common external tariff, the formation of the union will bring net welfare gain to the union as a whole and that (b) as the comparison is being made with the unopposed unilateral optimal trade policy for the home country, the home country's initial welfare position has been shown as being more favourable than would have been the case if the partner had also pursued its own optimum tariff policy.

From the global viewpoint, both the unilateral tariff policies of individual countries and the formation of customs unions are inevitably sub-optimal. Whilst the rest of the world is unable to react and co-operate with the home and partner countries to arrive at a globally optimal solution based on full international co-operation, the possibility exists for groups of countries to obtain aggregate benefit for themselves (partly at the expense of the rest of the world) by pursuing co-operation on a more limited scale.[1] From the global viewpoint, therefore, developments such as the formation of the customs union of the EEC and the hesitant steps towards regional monetary integration must be judged as desirable or not to the extent to which they either facilitate or prevent a wider international co-operation.

The 'large union' model has so far been exemplified by a very special case. It is easy to see, however, that the probability that the optimal common external tariff will be different from the optimal non-discriminatory tariff of the home country could be handled by an analysis which split the formation of the customs union into the two steps: (i), the adoption of the initial (optimal) tariff of the home country as the common external tariff and, (ii), the change in the common external tariff to the rate which is optimal from the viewpoint of the union as a whole. Step (i) would then involve the same kind of effects as shown in figure 5.1 but would not necessarily bring net gain to the union, whilst step (ii) would bring net gains which would modify the effects identified in step (i) without introducing any different sources of welfare change. The only interesting possibility suggested by the extension of the simple case already analysed is that ignorance or external constraints may prevent step (ii). In this case the common external tariff would not be optimal, so that the justification for the formation of the union would then depend on the empirical evaluation of trade creation, trade diversion and terms of trade effects. Equally, it can be acknowledged that the initial national tariff may not be optimal, and this possibility could also be taken into account by introducing the further step of considering the effects of the move from the initial tariff to the optimal non-discriminatory level. As in the 'small country' model, however, the gains accruing from such a step should not be attributed to economic integration unless there were effective constraints preventing such unilateral action.

So far the terms of trade argument for the formation of a customs union has been presented for the case in which the home country and partner may be termed 'complementary' or 'dissimilar' economies, in that their trade patterns are reversed, with the home country exporting commodity y and importing x whilst the partner exports x and imports y. Essentially the same kind of conclusions, however, also follow when the home country and the partner are presented as competitive economies which both export the same good. Again, the rationale for the formulation of the customs union rests upon the unwillingness or inability of the rest of the world to react to the actions of the home country and the partner or to co-operate with them in search of a globally optimal solution. Accordingly, the home country and the partner have the role of duopolists competing in the same market, the rest of the world. Various duopoly models exist of what might happen in such circumstances but, as is well known, the optimal policy from the combined viewpoint of the two duopolists is to co-operate by producing where their separate marginal costs are both equal to marginal revenue, thereby achieving the joint monopoly profit-maximising position. In the context of customs union theory, this is achieved by the home country and the partner removing mutual tariffs and by setting a common external tariff at the optimal rate, so as to equate the marginal value of importing into each of the member countries with the marginal cost of imports from the rest of the world. As in the previous case of complementary member economies, the formation of such a customs union brings both the benefits of free trade among members and the gains of exploiting their joint monopoly power in the face of a passive tariff policy in the rest of the world. Further, as recently shown by the empirical investigations of Petith (1977), the terms of trade effects of economic integration may well be of a significantly greater magnitude than trade creation and trade diversion effects, so that, although the latter determine the global welfare effect, it is the terms of trade gains which are likely to be more important for members of the union.

Summary

This outline of the orthodox framework of customs union theory presented in Chapters 2, 3, 4 and 5 suggests four principal conclusions. The first is that the rationale for regional economic integration rests upon the existence of constraints on the use of first best policy instruments. Thus, in the case of the 'large union' model, the optimality of regional economic integration depends upon the inability or unwillingness of the rest of the world to co-operate successfully with member countries in obtaining globally optimal solutions. In the 'small union' and 'small country' models, further constraints must be recognised – on the domestic use of first best policy instruments and on the unilateral use of export subsidies and preferential trade taxes. Economic analysis has had little to say about the nature of such constraints, and presumably the evaluation of any regional scheme of economic integration should incorporate a consideration of the validity of the view that such constraints do exist to justify the pursuit of second best rather than first best solutions.

Secondly, even when the existence of constraints on superior policy instruments is acknowledged, it is misleading to identify the results of regional economic integration by comparing an arbitrarily chosen common policy with an arbitrarily chosen national policy. Of course, ignorance and inertia provide sufficient reasons why existing policies may be non-optimal, but it is clearly wrong to attribute gains which would have been achieved by appropriate unilateral action to a policy of regional integration. Equally, although it is appropriate to use the optimal common policy as a point of reference, it must be recognised that this may overstate the gains to be achieved if, as seems highly likely, constraints and inefficiencies in the political processes by which policies are agreed prove to be greater among a group of countries than within any individual country.

Although the first two conclusions raise doubts about the case for regional economic integration, in principle, at least, a strong general case for economic integration does exist. As with the 'large union' model or the 'small union' model in which economies of scale may be in part external to national industries, this case rests essentially upon the recognition of the externalities and market imperfections which extend beyond the boundaries of national states. In such circumstances, unilateral national action will not be optimal, whilst integrated action offers the scope for potential gain.

As with the solution to most problems of externalities and market imperfections, however, customs union theory frequently illustrates the proposition that a major stumbling block to obtaining the gains from joint optimal action lies in agreeing an acceptable distribution of such gains. Thus, the fourth conclusion is that the achievement of the potential gains from economic integration will be limited to countries able and willing to co-operate to distribute the gains from integration so that all partners may benefit compared to the results achieved by independent action. (For a similar conclusion in the context of customs union for developing countries, see El-Agraa 1979b and Chapter 6.) It is easy to argue from this that regional economic integration may be more easily achieved than global solutions but, as the debate about monetary integration in the EEC illustrates, the chances of obtaining potential mutual gain may well founder in the presence of disparate views about the distribution of such gains and weak arrangements for redistribution.

Note

1 For a similar conclusion, derived by set-theoretical methods applied to a more general model incorporating many countries and commodities, see Kemp and Wan (1976).

6

Customs Unions in Developing Countries

A M EL-AGRAA[1]

The theory of economic integration has evolved, almost exclusively, from discussion of post Second World War European developments: the European Economic Community (EEC), the European Free Trade Association (EFTA) and COMECON – their Eastern European counterpart. The literature to date is certainly biased towards common markets in advanced economies – see the references cited by Lipsey (1960), Corden (1965) and Krauss (1972). This is in spite of the fact that the East African Common Market (EACM) was one of the pioneers in this field (see Due and Robson 1967, p. 533). One should emphasise, however, that the EACM was formed for colonial administrative convenience rather than as a voluntary association of independent nations (Hazelwood 1967).

The first rigorous attempt at a consideration of economic integration in the context of development was made by A.J. Brown (1961), and most of the subsequent work has concentrated on the estimate of the gains and losses from such associations – see Massell (1963), Newlyn (1965 and 1966),[2] Hazelwood (1966, 1967 and 1975), Wood (1966), Ghai (1967), Robson (1968) and Kahnert *et al.* (1969). The most notable exceptions are the contributions by the late H.G. Johnson (1965)[3] and by Cooper and Massell (1965b).

This chapter develops a three-country version of the model used by Brown to highlight some of his conclusions and to add a significant new conclusion. The theory of economic integration and development in particular and of economic integration in general will then be examined in the light of this new conclusion.

The Theory of Economic Integration[4]

It used to be the accepted tradition that economic integration is beneficial and should be encouraged. The logic behind this ran thus: free trade maximises world welfare; a customs union is a move towards free trade; a customs union therefore increases world welfare, even though it does not maximise it. Viner (1950) challenged this tradition by pointing to the harmful 'trade diversion' effects of a customs union. He emphasised that trade diversion should be compared with trade creation before an economic judgement can be passed on a customs union. Cooper and Massell (1965a) then demonstrated that a unilateral tariff reduction will always be superior to a customs union.

Developments from there on took two different paths. Johnson (1965) reversed the Vinerian conclusion: trade diversion is beneficial for the countries concerned while trade creation may be good or bad – see Chapter 7. The other developments centred on the terms of trade effects (Arndt 1968 and Petith 1977) and the (so-called) dynamic effects – Balassa (1962) and Scitovsky (1958) were the first to use the term in the context of economic integration; Corden (1972) shows that scale economies can easily be tackled within the traditional framework – see Chapter 3. Cooper and Massell (1965b) demonstrated that two countries acting together can do better than each acting alone – this conclusion is not as clear cut as is suggested here because one of the necessary pre-conditions is that non-optimum tariffs are being used (see Chapter 3).

As far as developing countries are concerned, it was immediately realised (see Meade 1956, Lipsey 1960 and Brown 1961) that the static resource reallocation effects have little relevance. The theory suggested that there would be more scope for trade creation if the countries concerned were initially very competitive in production but potentially very complementary and that a customs union would be more likely to be 'trade creating' if the partners conducted most of their foreign trade amongst themselves. These conditions are unlikely to be satisfied in the majority of the developing nations. Moreover, most of the effects of integration are bound to be 'trade diverting', since most developing countries seek to industrialise.

On the other hand, it was also realised that an important obstacle to the development of industry in the less developed nations is the inadequate size of their individual markets – see Brown (1961), Hazelwood (1967 and 1975) and Metwally (1979). It is, therefore, necessary to increase the market size so as to encourage optimum plant installations – hence the need for economic integration. This would, however, result in industries clustering together in the relatively more advanced of these nations – those that have already commenced the process of industrialisation; this is the so-called 'back-wash' effect discussed by Brown (1961), Hazelwood (1975) and Robson (1969).

Brown, using a two-country model, argued that even though the clustering together of industries might be a natural development, the other parties to the union would gain from such an association and that the benefits could be more equitably distributed if some fiscal arrangements were introduced for this purpose; this is the so-called 'spread' or multiplier effect discussed by Brown (1961).

These developments have led to the conclusion that economic integration in the advanced world is a very different matter from that in the developing world – see Hazelwood (1975), Robson (1969) and Kahnert *et al.* (1969). This conclusion is examined in this chapter by a three-country version of Brown's model.

A Three-Country Version of Brown's Model

In order to simplify the analysis I shall (as did Brown) assume the following:

(a) Factors of production are perfectly mobile within each country but lack the freedom to move across national borders. The union is, therefore, not allowed to introduce measures to divert resources to the industrialising partner. Hence, the union is necessarily a customs union rather than a common market; in a common market there should be free factor mobility across the borders of partner countries – see the Introduction to this book;

(b) There is a plentiful unutilised supply of all factors of production;

(c) The newly introduced industrial output is to be sold as a substitute for a product imported from the rest of the world; hence, the customs union is purely trade diverting. This product will be sold at a price equal to the import price plus the customs duty – this amounts to assuming that the customs union has an external tariff rate equal to the initial (equal) rate(s);

(d) Each of the partner nations receives customs revenue from those commodities which are consumed within its territories as well as the revenue from direct and excise taxes collected accordingly;

(e) The governments' budgets are to remain balanced throughout, so that any change in government revenue must bring about an equal change in government expenditure. This change in expenditure must fall on goods and services so that transfers are unaltered;

(f) No change in investment takes place in any of the partner countries. This might seem a very strange assumption, particularly when a new industrial output is to be introduced. It will become apparent, however, that the relaxation of this assumption will reinforce the conclusions of the analysis rather than render them invalid.

The newly produced output of manufactured goods by the partner that has already commenced industrialisation will be indicated by P. The tax-free value of the imports displaced by this new product is $P(1 - t)$, where t is the *ad valorem* marginal rate of duty in the three partner countries: 1, 2 and 3. Country 1 is the partner that has already started industrialising.

x_1 and x_2 of P are consumed in countries 1 and 2 respectively while the remainder $P(1 - x_1 - x_2)$ is consumed in country 3. Thus the consumption of P in countries 2 and 3 together is equal to $P(1 - x_1)$.

m_1, m_2 and m_3 are the total marginal propensities to import (mpi) of countries 1, 2 and 3 respectively. These mpi are composed of three parts each: a_1, a_2 and $[m_1 - (a_1 + a_2)]$ are country 1's mpi from countries 2, 3 and the rest of the world respectively; a_3, a_4 and $[m_2 - (a_3 + a_4)]$ are country 2's mpi from countries 1, 3 and the rest of the world respectively, and; a_5, a_6 and $[m_3 - (a_5 + a_6)]$ are the mpi of country 3 from 1, 2 and the rest of the world respectively.

t^* is the direct marginal tax rate.

The change in income in each country due to the newly introduced industrial output is measured in each country by:

$$Y = C + Td + X - M$$[5]

where Y is the change in income at factor cost, C is the change in consumption at market price, Td is the change in direct tax revenue, X is the change in exports at market price and M is the change in imports at factor cost.

The change in direct tax revenue is related to the change in income by t^*, the direct marginal tax rate $(Td = t^*Y)$. Consumption is related to disposable income by c, the marginal propensity to consume (mpc) $[C = c(Y - Td) = cY(1 - t^*)]$.

Td appears in the equation because the change in consumption expenditure is related to disposable income. Hence, the government must receive income tax revenue. Since it is assumed that the budget is balanced, tax receipts must be spent on goods and services. Therefore, *Td* represents the government sector.

There are two parts to the change in country 1's exports. The first part is equal to x_2P and $P(1 - x_1 - x_2)$, the sum of the two being $(1 - x_1)P$. This represents the substitution of part of the newly produced industrial output in country 1 for imports from the rest of the world in countries 2 and 3. The second part is equal to $a_3\ Y_2$ and $a_t Y_3$. These represent the increased exports to countries 2 and 3 induced by their respective income changes.

There are also two parts to the change in imports in country 1: an increase equal to $m_1 Y_1$ due to the increased income in the country, and a reduction equal to $x_1 P(1-t)$ which is the consequence of country 1's substitution of a proportion of the new industrial output for imports from the rest of the world.

Taking all this into account, plus the consumption and the direct tax receipts changes, one gets:

$$Y_1 = \frac{a_3 Y_2 + a_5 Y_3 + P(1 - x_1 t_1)}{s_1(1 - t_1^*) + m_1} \quad (1)$$

For country 2 the change in exports is equal to $a_1 Y_1$ and $a_6 Y_3$, which are the exports induced by the income changes in countries 1 and 3 respectively. The change in imports is equal to $m_2 Y_2$, which is the increased imports in country 2 induced by its income change, and tx_2P, which is the amount of import duty previously collected from imports coming from the rest of the world now replaced by imports from country 1. This customs revenue is now received by country 1 as part of the price of the proportion of P consumed in country 2 (assumption c).

This gives:

$$Y_2 = \frac{a_1 Y_1 + a_6 Y_3 - t_2 x_2 P}{s_2(1 - t_2^*) + m_2} \quad (2)$$

Following exactly the same procedure as in the case of country 2, one can derive the income change for country 3. Thus, the change in exports is equal to $a_2 Y_1$ and $a_4 Y_2$, and the change in imports is equal to $m_3 Y_3$ and $t_3 P(1 - x_1 - x_2)$. Hence:

$$Y_3 = \frac{a_2 Y_1 + a_4 Y_2 - t_3 P(1 - x_1 - x_2)}{s_3(1 - t_3^*) + m_3} \quad (3)$$

These equations are untidy in their present form, particularly since one is interested in the income changes in terms of P alone. Eliminating the irrelevant income changes gives:

$$Y_1 = \frac{M(b_2 b_3 - a_4 a_6) + N(a_4 a_5 + a_3 b_3) + K(a_3 a_6 + a_5 b_2)}{D} \quad (1')$$

$$Y_2 = \frac{M(a_2 a_6 + a_1 b_3) + N(b_1 b_3 - a_2 a_5) + K(a_1 a_5 + a_6 b_1)}{D} \quad (2')$$

and

$$Y_3 = \frac{M(a_1 a_4 + a_2 b_3) + N(a_2 a_3 + a_4 b_1) + K(b_1 b_2 - a_1 a_3)}{D} \quad (3')$$

where:

$$\begin{aligned}
D &= b_1 b_2 b_3 - a_4 a_6 b_1 - a_1 a_3 b_3 - a_1 a_4 a_5 - a_2 a_3 a_6 - a_2 a_5 b_2\,;\\
M &= P(1 - x_1 t_1)\,;\\
N &= - t_2 x_2 P\,;\\
K &= - t_3 P(1 - x_1 - x_2)\,;\\
b_1 &= s_1 (1 - t_1^*) + m_1\,;\\
b_2 &= s_2 (1 - t_2^*) + m_2\,;\\
b_3 &= s_3 (1 - t_3^*) + m_3\,.
\end{aligned}$$

Equations (1′) – (3′) can be used to formulate the net spill-over ratios:[6]

$$\frac{Y_2}{Y_1} = \frac{M(a_2 a_6 + a_1 b_3) + N(b_1 b_3 - a_2 a_5) + K(a_1 a_5 + a_6 b_1)}{M(b_2 b_3 - a_4 a_6) + N(a_4 a_5 + a_3 b_3) + K(a_3 a_6 + a_5 b_2)}\,; \quad (4)$$

$$\frac{Y_3}{Y_1} = \frac{M(a_1 a_4 + a_2 b_2) + N(a_2 a_3 + a_4 b_1) + K(b_1 b_2 - a_1 a_3)}{M(b_2 b_3 - a_4 a_6) + N(a_4 a_5 + a_3 b_3) + K(a_3 a_6 + a_5 b_2)}\,; \quad (5)$$

and

$$\frac{Y_2}{Y_3} = \frac{M(a_2 a_6 + a_1 b_3) + N(b_1 b_3 - a_2 a_5) + K(a_1 a_5 + a_6 b_1)}{M(a_1 a_4 + a_2 b_2) + N(a_2 a_3 + a_4 b_1) + K(b_1 b_2 - a_1 a_3)}\,. \quad (6)$$

These equations are mathematically too complicated to handle. To make deductions from them I shall insert some hypothetical but representative values.[7] The data are given in table 6.1 and the resulting income changes in table 6.2.

These results lead to the following conclusions:

Table 6.1 *Representative Data*

Variable	t_1	t_2	t_3	t_1^*	t_2^*	t_3^*	s_1	s_2	s_3	a_1	a_2	a_3	a_4	a_5	a_6	m_1	m_2	m_3	x_1	x_2	$1-x_1-x_2$
Case I	0.2	0.2	0.2	0.1	0.1	0.1	0.15	0.15	0.15	0.05	0.05	0.05	0.05	0.05	0.05	0.3	0.3	0.3	0.75	0.125	0.125
	0.2	0.1	0.2	0.1	0.05	0.1	0.15	0.1	0.15	0.1	0.1	0.1	0.1	0.1	0.1	0.35	0.3	0.3	0.75	0.25	0.0
	0.3	0.2	0.2	0.2	0.1	0.1	0.2	0.15	0.15	0.05	0.05	0.1	0.05	0.05	0.05	0.3	0.35	0.3	0.5	0.25	0.25
	0.2	0.3	0.2	0.1	0.2	0.1	0.15	0.2	0.15	0.05	0.05	0.05	0.1	0.05	0.05				0.8	0.1	0.1
	0.3	0.3	0.3	0.2	0.2	0.2	0.2	0.2	0.2	0.05	0.05	0.0	0.05	0.05	0.05						
		Cases XIX–XXII			Cases XV–XVIII			Cases XI–XIV					Cases II–V				Cases VI and VIII			Cases VIII–X	

Note: Case I is the basic case; all other cases have the same values for their variables except for the variables specified. For each category, the case number is to be read from top to bottom.

Table 6.2 *Results*

Result / Case	$Y_1 = P$	$Y_2 = P$	$Y_3 = P$	$\frac{Y_2}{Y_1}$	$\frac{Y_3}{Y_1}$	$\frac{Y_2}{Y_1}$
I	1.999	0.195	0.195	0.097	0.097	1.000
II	2.225	0.590	0.590	0.265	0.265	1.000
III	2.022	0.198	0.198	0.098	0.098	1.000
IV	2.002	0.198	0.218	0.099	0.109	0.097
V	1.976	0.192	0.192	0.097	0.097	1.000
VI	1.787	0.167	0.167	0.094	0.094	1.000
VII	1.996	0.174	0.192	0.087	0.096	0.907
VIII	1.999	0.143	0.246	0.072	0.123	0.581
IX	2.102	0.143	0.143	0.068	0.068	1.000
X	1.978	0.205	0.205	0.104	0.104	1.000
XI	2.002	0.218	0.198	0.109	0.099	1.102
XII	1.806	0.170	0.170	0.094	0.094	1.000
XIII	1.996	0.176	0.192	0.088	0.096	0.915
XIV	1.802	0.151	0.151	0.084	0.084	1.000
XV	1.998	0.191	0.194	0.096	0.097	0.985
XVI	2.072	0.204	0.204	0.099	0.099	1.000
XVII	2.000	0.202	0.196	0.101	0.098	1.032
XVIII	2.074	0.213	0.213	0.103	0.103	1.000
XIX	2.003	0.224	0.198	0.112	0.099	1.130
XX	1.821	0.172	0.172	0.094	0.094	1.000
XXI	1.995	0.165	0.191	0.083	0.096	0.865
XXII	1.813	0.138	0.138	0.076	0.076	1.000

(a) Y_1 is a multiple of the newly introduced industrial output (the results range from $2.225P$ to $1.787P$) while Y_2 and Y_3 are a small but positive fraction of it (the results range from $0.59P$ to $0.143P$). These results are clearly indicated by the net spill-over ratios, which range from 0.072 to 0.265 (7–25 per cent).[8]

(b) Cases II–VII, considered together, clearly indicate that the higher (the lower) the three countries' marginal propensities to import from each other, the higher (the lower) the income changes, and the higher (the lower) their marginal propensities to import from the rest of the world, the lower (the higher) the resulting income changes (Cases VI and VII).[9]

Within this general conclusion one notices the following:

(i) the higher (the lower) the marginal propensities of the three countries to import from each other, the higher (the lower) the rates of change of the income changes for countries 2 and 3 (Case II). In other words, the net spill-over ratios are at their highest (lowest);

(ii) the higher (the lower) the marginal propensity of country 2 (3) to import from country 1, the higher (the lower) the income change over all. This income change is, however, experienced equally by country 3 (2) – [Cases II and V]. This suggests the result that one would expect: *the crucial factor is the marginal propensity of country 1 to import from the other two countries;*[10]

(iii) the higher (the lower) country 2's marginal propensity to import from country 3, the higher (the lower) the income change in country 3 and the lower the rate of change of income change in country 1 (Case IV) – this result is consistent with the previous conclusion and, of course, with the concept of the multiplier in general.

(c) As one would expect, the higher (the lower) the marginal propensities to save, the lower (the higher) the income changes (Cases XI–XIV). Also the higher (the lower) the income tax rates, the higher (the lower) the income changes (Cases XV–XVIII). This is clearly suggested by the definitional expressions.[11] Moreover, the higher (the lower) the tariff rates, the lower (the higher) the income changes – this follows from assumption (c): the higher the tariff rate, the greater the loss to 2 and 3 from such a union.

(d) The most significant conclusion is that the lower (the higher) the proportion of the newly introduced industrial output consumed by a partner, the higher (the lower) that country's income change (Cases VIII – X). The importance of this conclusion will be discussed in the following section.

Interpretation of the Conclusions

Most of these conclusions are quite consistent with Brown's except for the generalisations made possible by the use of a three-country model. Conclusion (d) is, however, not mentioned by him.[12] Here, country 3 (2) decides not to partake in this union (Case VIII). This decision is reflected in its continuing to import from the outside world rather than consume any part of the newly introduced industrial product. As a result, country 3 experiences an income change much larger than it would as a member of the union (Case I). The income change is $0.246P$ as against $0.195P$, giving a net spill-over ratio of 0.123 as against 0.097.

This result can be shown mathematically. Suppose that country 3 decides not to partake in this common market, then:

For Y_1, the components are as before. Hence

$$Y_1 = \frac{a_3 Y_2 + a_5 Y_3 + P(1 - x_1 t_1)}{s_1(1 - t_1^*) + m_1} \tag{1}$$

For Y_2, M_2 becomes:

$$m_2 Y_2 + t(1 - x_1)P$$

all the other components remaining the same as before. Hence

$$Y_2 = \frac{a_1 Y_1 + a_6 Y_3 - t_2 P(1 - x_1)}{s_2(1 - t_2^*) + m_2} \tag{7}$$

For Y_3, M_3 becomes:

$$m_3 Y_3$$

all the other components remaining the same. Hence

$$Y_3 = \frac{a_2 Y_1 + a_4 Y_2}{s_3(1 - t_3^*) + m_3} \tag{8}$$

Comparing (8) and (3) it is obvious that Y_3 as given by (8) is greater than Y_3 as given by equation (3) by a multiple of

$$t_3 P(1 - x_1 - x_2).$$

The multiplier is given by

$$\frac{1}{s_3(1 - t_3^*) + m_3}$$

The point that needs emphasising, therefore, is that *the crucial consideration is not whether or not Y_2 and Y_3 would be negative or positive, but whether or not they would have been greater had countries 2 and 3 decided to stay out of the union.* The results clearly show that countries 2 and 3 are better off staying out of this association.

Could one then argue [from conclusion b(ii)] that since it is country 1's marginal propensity to import from 2 and 3 which is the most significant element, then it is to the benefit of 2 and 3 to join a union with 1? It is quite obvious that such an argument would be absurd – these 'spread' effects are the outcome of the three countries' normal relationships (apart from this new industrial output) and unless country 1 suddenly decides to exercise some compulsion on 2 and 3, there is no reason why these normal relationships should be disturbed. Moreover, it is to the benefit of country 1 to have a market for disposing of its surplus industrial output.

Hence, both these considerations point to the fact that it is country 1 which benefits most from this association.

A Reappraisal

I have demonstrated that there is no economic justification for a customs union of developing countries based on protected industrialisation, i.e. a trade diverting association – see Chapter 2 for a more specific definition. One could of course argue that such a union would be desirable if fiscal arrangements were established with the aim of distributing the gains equitably or of locating the industries in a more scattered fashion [indeed, Brown (p. 91) determines the income changes for the partner countries in the situation when there is a common pooling of revenues and their distribution; the equivalent equations for the three-country model can easily be worked out but they are really not relevant to the argument in this chapter]. Both would be reasonable suggestions but they are not of direct relevance here – see Chapter 3.

My immediate concern is with the proposition that the theory of economic integration as developed for the advanced world has very little relevance to the developing world. Ignoring the subtle issues raised in Chapters 2, 3 and 4, there are three basic considerations for a *purely* economic justification of customs unions: (i) the static resource reallocation effects, i.e. the trade creation and trade diversion effects, (ii) the terms of trade effects and (iii) the (so-called) dynamic effects – economies of scale and external economies. I have demonstrated in this chapter that there is no difference between advanced and developing nations as far as (i) is concerned: trade diversion is bad because the country concerned is bound to lose (a *multiple* of the loss of) its tariff revenue.

As for the terms of trade effects, these can come about only if the members of the union can charge higher export prices and/or bargain for lower import prices. Here one is thrown into the world of monopoly/monopsony or oligopoly/oligopsony where any outcome is perfectly feasible, particularly if retaliation by the injured parties is allowed for (see Arndt 1968, Petith 1977 (who finds evidence for terms of trade improvements in the EEC but specifies that no retaliation has, in fact, occurred during the period examined) and my 1979 articles). I cannot, however, see any differences between advanced and developing countries in this respect, and, if the immediate past is anything to go by, it is the OPEC countries that seem to have gained from such action. Needless to say, OPEC is not a customs union.

As for scale economies, it is equally obvious that there is more scope for them in a union of developing countries than in the EEC or in EFTA; they are the basic necessity for integration and development. Indeed, it has been argued quite coherently that it is the market size that is an important factor in economic development – see Brown 1963, Hazelwood 1967 and 1975, and Mikesell 1960. Moreover, the discussion between Professors Johnson and Williamson (1962) has questioned that there is great scope for scale economies in the EEC – see Johnson 1957 and 1958, Williamson 1971 and Brown 1963.

When it comes to external economies, it is also obvious that there is much more scope for them (and absolute need for them for development purposes) in the developing countries than in the advanced world: a pool of skilled labour, the provision of technology and infrastructure are the basic necessities of industry and they are lacking.

It therefore appears that the body of theory developed for economic integration in the advanced world is more *appropriate* for the developing countries.

Conclusion

This chapter supports Johnson's (see also Chapters 3 and 8) preference for a political economy approach to economic integration. It also claims that there is *essentially no theoretical difference* between economic integration in the advanced world and in the developing world. However, there is a major difference in terms of the type of economic integration (see the Introduction and Balassa 1962) that is politically feasible; the need for an equitable distribution of the gains from industrialisation and the location of industries is an important issue. This suggests that any type of economic integration that is being contemplated must incorporate as an essential element a common fiscal authority and some co-ordination of economic policies. But then one could equally well argue that *some degree* of these elements is necessary in any type of integration – see the recommendations of the Raisman Committee (1961) for the East African Common Market.

Notes

1 This chapter is based on my essay with a similar title which is published in J.K. Bowers (ed.), *Inflation, Development and Integration: Essays in Honour of A.J. Brown*, Leeds University Press 1979. I am grateful to the editor for giving me permission to draw very heavily on that essay.

2 Newlyn's (1965) contribution contains some interesting ideas on the methodology of estimating these gains and losses, for example, his concept of the 'shiftability' of industry.

3 The ideas put forward in this article are general enough to cover integration at all levels of economic development. No reference to this article is made in any of the literature on economic integration and development. It must be added, however, that it has made little impact on the theory of economic integration in developed countries – see Chapter 7.

4 For a comprehensive survey of the literature see Lipsey (1960), Corden (1965), and Krauss (1972) and Chapters 2–5 of this book.

5 '. . . since that part of extra government expenditure which is financed by indirect taxation is offset by the subtraction of the extra revenue required to reduce income to a factor cost basis,' A.J. Brown, Economic separatism *versus* a common market in developing countries, *Bulletin of Economic Research*, vol. 13, 1961, p. 89. Expressed in symbols:

$Y_{f.c.} + M_{f.c.} + Ti = C_{m.p.} + G_{m.p.} + X_{m.p.}$ (i) where $G_{m.p.} = Ti + Td$ (ii). Substituting (ii) into (i), simplifying and arranging, one gets: $Y_{f.c.} = C_{m.p.} + Td + X_{m.p.} - M_{f.c.}$.

6 The term 'net spill-over ratio' was coined by Newlyn in his 1966 article, p. 131.

7 The hypothetical data is consistent with that used by Brown in his article (*op. cit.*), and is subject to the same limitations cited there. I have, however, chosen a range of values so that most possible situations can be examined.

8 This result is clearly consistent with Brown's '. . . the country in which manufacturing arises to displace imports into the free trade area experiences a rise in income equal to twice the new manufactured output, the rest of the area experiences a rise in income equal to about a tenth of the new manufactured output' (p. 90).

9 This result is also clearly specified by Brown:'. . . the higher this marginal propensity to import, the greater *B*'s share in the total income increase for the free trade area' (p. 91).

10 Brown calculates the crucial value for country 1's marginal propensity to import from country 2 (and 3 here) – this is the value for a_1 and a_2 which produces $Y_2 (= Y_3)$ equal to zero. The equivalent values for the model used in this chapter are given in

the Appendix table 1. They are not discussed at length at this stage for reasons that will shortly become apparent and also because it 'does not seem very likely that the marginal propensity of one country to import from a neighbour to which it is bound in a free trade area will be so small as to bring about this result'. Brown, p. 91.

11 This is because any income tax revenue is spent by the government to counteract the effect of the difference between 'earned' and 'disposable' income on consumption. But it is well known that a government expenditure financed by equal taxation has a multiplier effect, particularly in such a highly simplified model.

12 Brown does hint at the conclusion but in a different context: 'though the chance of 'country B' actually losing national income as a result of A's development is small . . . the chance of its government losing revenue is somewhat greater. There is a direct loss of customs revenue equal to $tc(1 - x)P$', Brown, *op. cit.*, p. 91.

It is apparent from the main text that the actual loss must be a multiple of that loss in tariff revenue.

Appendix *Table 1*

Critical a_1 and a_2 Values to Produce (i) $Y_2 = 0$ (ii) $Y_3 = 0$ (iii) $Y_2 = Y_3 = 0$

	$Y_2 = 0$ $a = a_1$	$Y_3 = 0$ $a = a_2$	$Y_2 = Y_3 = 0$ $a_1 = a_2 =$	a_2 if not equal to a_1
I	0.0084	0.0084	0.0128	
II	−0.0079	−0.0079	0.0128	
III	0.0084	0.0082	0.0128	
IV	0.0084	0.0041	0.0128	
V	0.0084	0.0085	0.0128	
VI	0.0100	0.0100	0.0143	
VII	0.0084	0.0088	0.0128	
VIII	0.0195	−0.0028	0.0256	−0.0000
IX	0.0210	0.0210	0.0242	
X	0.0057	0.0057	0.0104	
XI	0.0084	0.0079	0.0128	
XII	0.0099	0.0099	0.0141	
XIII	0.0084	0.0088	0.0128	
XIV	0.0103	0.0106	0.0141	
XV	0.0084	0.0085	0.0128	
XVI	0.0079	0.0079	0.0124	
XVII	0.0084	0.0082	0.0128	
XVIII	0.0077	0.0077	0.0124	
XIX	0.0020	0.0076	0.0064	0.0128
XX	0.0098	0.0095	0.0140	
XXI	0.0147	0.0091	0.0192	
XXII	0.0175	0.0175	0.0211	

7

Macroeconomics of Trade Creation and Trade Diversion

A M EL-AGRAA

Trade creation and trade diversion are the two concepts that are most widely used in international economic integration.[1] Their economic implications for resource reallocation are usually tackled in terms of particular commodities under conditions of full employment in the countries forming the customs union.[2] The economic consequences for the outside world and their repercussions on the customs union partners are usually left to intuition.[3]

The purpose of this chapter is to attempt to fill this gap in the literature of international economic integration. The discussion is based on two of my papers[4] which use a macro-economic approach to tackle this problem.

The Model

In order to simplify the analysis I shall assume that:

(a) Factors of production are perfectly mobile within each country but are not allowed to move across national frontiers.

(b) Unutilised factor supplies exist in the country where they are required.

(c) Each country receives customs revenue from those commodities which are consumed within its territories as well as the revenue from direct excise taxes.

(d) The governments' budgets are to remain balanced throughout, so that any change in government revenue must bring about an equal change in government expenditure. This change in expenditure must fall on goods and services so that transfers remain unaltered.
(e) There is no change in investment as a result of trade creation, i.e. no expenditure on plant and equipment is necessary for the production of the new exports in the partner country concerned.
(f) Prices are to remain constant throughout the analysis.

The Initial Situation

In the situation before the establishment of the customs union, national income in each country is determined in the usual fashion:

$$Y = C + I + G + X - M$$

where Y, C, I, G, X and M stand for national income, planned consumption expenditure, planned investment expenditure, planned government expenditure, planned exports and planned imports respectively.

Since any change in any of the components of Y will lead to a change in Y, it follows that:

$$dY = dC + dI + dG + dX - dM \quad (1)$$

where d indicates a change in the relevant element.

Now, specify these elements for each of the three countries:

$$dC_1 = c_1 dY_1(1 - t_1) \quad (2)$$
$$dC_2 = c_2 dY_2(1 - t_2) \quad (3)$$
$$dC_3 = c_3 dY_3(1 - t_3) \quad (4)$$

where c is the marginal propensity to consume, t is the marginal income tax rate,[5] 1 and 2 are the potential customs union partners and 3 stands for the outside world. These expressions state that any change in planned consumption expenditure is attributed to a change in disposable income in the country under consideration.

Also:

$$\begin{aligned} dM_1 &= m_{12}dY_1(1+t_1^*) + m_{13}dY_1(1+t_1^*) \\ &= dY_1(m_{12}+m_{13})(1+t_1^*) \end{aligned} \tag{5}$$

$$\begin{aligned} dM_2 &= m_{21}dY_2(1+t_2^*) + m_{23}dY_2(1+t_2) \\ &= dY_2(m_{21}+m_{23})(1+t_2^*) \end{aligned} \tag{6}$$

$$\begin{aligned} dM_3 &= m_{31}dY_3(1+t_3^*) + m_{32}dY_3(1+t_3^*) \\ &= dY_3(m_{31}+m_{32})(1+t_3^*) \end{aligned} \tag{7}$$

where t^* is the *ad valorem* rate of customs duty and m is the marginal propensity to import with the subscripts read in the orthodox fashion. For example, m_{32} is the marginal propensity of country 3 to import from country 2.[6]

Since one country's imports are another country's exports, it follows that:

$$dX_1 = m_{21}dY_2 + m_{31}dY_3 \tag{8}$$
$$dX_2 = m_{12}dY_1 + m_{32}dY_3 \tag{9}$$
$$dX_3 = m_{13}dY_1 + m_{23}dY_2 \tag{10}$$

Substituting these definitional equations into the income changes and assuming that governments' budgets remain balanced, we get:

$$\begin{aligned} dY_1 &= c_1dY_1(1-t_1) + dI_1 + m_{21}dY_2 \\ &\quad + m_{31}dY_3 + t_1dY_1 + t_1^*dY_1(m_{12}+m_{13}) \\ &\quad - dY_1(m_{12}+m_{13})(1+t_1^*) \end{aligned} \tag{11}$$

$$\begin{aligned} dY_2 &= c_2dY_2(1-t_2) + dI_2 + m_{12}dY_1 \\ &\quad + m_{32}dY_3 + t_2dY_2 + t_2^*dY_2(m_{21}+m_{23}) \\ &\quad - dY_2(m_{21}+m_{23})(1+t_2^*) \end{aligned} \tag{12}$$

$$\begin{aligned} dY_3 &= c_3dY_3(1-t_3) + dI_3 + m_{13}dY_1 \\ &\quad + m_{23}dY_2 + t_3dY_3 + t_3^*dY_3(m_{31}+m_{32}) \\ &\quad - dY_3(m_{31}+m_{32})(1+t_3^*) \end{aligned} \tag{13}$$

These equations can be simplified to give:

$$dY_1 = \frac{m_{21}dY_2 + m_{31}dY_3 + dI_1}{s_1(1-t_1) + m_{12} + m_{13}} \tag{11'}$$

$$dY_2 = \frac{m_{12}dY_1 + m_{32}dY_3 + dI_2}{s_2(1-t_2) + m_{21} + m_{23}} \tag{12'}$$

$$dY_3 = \frac{m_{13}dY_1 + m_{23}dY_2 + dI_3}{s_3(1-t_3) + m_{31} + m_{32}} \tag{13'}$$

where $s = 1 - c$.

These equations are untidy in their present form, particularly since one is interested in expressing the income changes only in terms of the income change in the country concerned. The income changes for the three countries are:[7]

$$dY_1 = \frac{dI_1(b_2b_3 - m_{23}m_{32}) + dI_2(m_{21}b_3 + m_{23}m_{31}) + dI_3(m_{21}m_{32} + m_{31}b_2)}{D} \tag{14}$$

$$dY_2 = \frac{dI_1(m_{13}m_{32} + m_{12}b_3) + dI_2(b_1b_3 - m_{13}m_{31}) + dI_3(m_{12}m_{31} + m_{32}b_1)}{D} \tag{15}$$

$$dY_3 = \frac{dI_1(m_{12}m_{23} + m_{13}b_2) + dI_2(m_{13}m_{21} + m_{23}b_1) + dI_3(b_1b_2 - m_{12}m_{21})}{D} \tag{16}$$

where:

$$\begin{aligned} b_1 &= s_1(1-t_1) + m_{12} + m_{13} \\ b_2 &= s_2(1-t_2) + m_{21} + m_{23} \\ b_3 &= s_3(1-t_3) + m_{31} + m_{32} \\ D &= b_1b_2b_3 - m_{23}m_{32}b_1 - m_{12}m_{21}b_3 - m_{12}m_{23}m_{31} \\ &\quad - m_{13}m_{21}m_{32} - m_{13}m_{31}b_2 \end{aligned}$$

Equations (14)–(16) give a meaningful expression of the state of interdependence between the three countries in the initial situation of non-discriminatory protection. They are expressions of the multiplier relationships with foreign repercussions. These equations can, therefore, be used to study the effect an autonomous change in investment (which could be taken to represent a change in *any* autonomous element) in any of the three countries would have on any or all of them.

Trade Creation

The initial state of interdependence in this international economy of three countries is expressed in equations (14)–(16). Let us examine the impact of the formation of a purely trade-creating customs union (see Chapter 2 for a specific definition) between countries 1 and 2 on these initial interrelationships.

The establishment of the customs union results in the removal of tariff barriers between 1 and 2. Trade creation means that a certain quantity of output (q) that is initially produced domestically in country 1 is now to be imported from country 2. The original value of this output is qp_1 where p_1 is the price in country 1. The new value of this output is qp_2 where p_2 is the price in country 2. Trade creation means that $qp_1 > qp_2$, i.e. $p_1 > p_2$.

Trade creation results in the following expressions:

$$\begin{aligned} dY_1^* = {} & c_1 dY_1^*(1 - t_1) + dI_1 + m_{21} dY_2^* \\ & + m_{31} dY_3^* + t_1 dY_1^* + t_1^* dY_1^* m_{13} - qp_1 \\ & - (dY_1^* m_{13} + qp_2) - dY_1^* m_{13}(1 + t_1^*) \end{aligned} \tag{17}$$

$$\begin{aligned} dY_2^* = {} & c_2 dY_2^*(1 - t_2) + dI_2 + m_{12} dY_1^* \\ & + m_{32} dY_3^* + qp_2 + t_2 dY_2^* \\ & + t_2^* dY_2^* m_{23} - dY_2^* m_{21} - dY_2^* m_{23}(1 + t_2^*) \end{aligned} \tag{18}$$

$$\begin{aligned} dY_3^* = {} & c_3 dY_3^*(1 - t_3) + dI_3 + m_{13} dY_1^* \\ & + m_{23} dY_2^* + t_3 dY_3^* + t_3 dY_3^*(m_{31} + m_{32}) \\ & - dY_3^*(m_{31} + m_{32})(1 + t_3^*) \end{aligned} \tag{19}$$

where t^* is the *ad valorem* rate of customs duty and Y^* is the new income change. These expressions can be simplified:

$$dY_1^* = \frac{m_{21} dY_2^* + m_{31} dY_3^* + dI_1 - q(p_1 + p_2)}{b_1} \tag{20}$$

$$dY_2^* = \frac{m_{12} dY_1 + m_{32} dY_3^* + dI_2 + qp_2}{b_2} \tag{21}$$

$$dY_3^* = \frac{m_{13} dY_1^* + m_{23} dY_2^* + dI_3}{b_3} \tag{22}$$

Equations (20)–(22) can be expressed in a form equivalent to equations (14)–(16). Hence:

$$\begin{aligned} dY_1^* = \{&[dI_1 - q(p_1 + p_2)](b_2 b_3 - m_{23} m_{32}) \\ &+ (dI_2 + q p_2)(m_{21} b_3 + m_{23} m_{31}) \\ &+ dI_3(m_{21} m_{32} + m_{31} b_2)\}/D \end{aligned} \tag{20'}$$

$$\begin{aligned} dY_2^* = \{&[dI_1 - q(p_1 + p_2)](m_{13} m_{32} + m_{12} b_3) \\ &+ (dI_2 + q p_2)(b_1 b_3 - m_{13} m_{31}) \\ &+ dI_3(m_{12} m_{31} + m_{32} b_1)\}/D \end{aligned} \tag{21'}$$

$$\begin{aligned} dY_3^* = \{&[dI_1 - q(p_1 + p_2)](m_{12} m_{23} + m_{13} b_2) \\ &+ (dI_2 + q p_2)(m_{13} m_{21} + m_{23} b_1) \\ &+ dI_3(b_1 b_2 - m_{12} m_{21})\}/D \end{aligned} \tag{22'}$$

These expressions make it possible to assess the effects of trade creation on the three countries. Comparing the initial situation depicted by equations (14)–(16) with the customs union inter-relationships given by equations (20′)–(22′), it can be seen that: If

$q p_2(m_{21} b_3 + m_{23} m_{31}) > q(p_1 + p_2)(b_2 b_3 - m_{23} m_{32})$, then $dY_1^* > dY_1$

q can be eliminated from this condition. Hence:

If $p_2(m_{21} b_3 + m_{23} m_{31}) > (p_1 + p_2)(b_2 b_3 - m_{23} m_{32})$, then $dy_1^* > dY_1$ (23)

If $p_2(b_1 b_3 - m_{13} m_{31}) > (p_1 + p_2)(m_{13} m_{32} + m_{12} b_3)$, then $dY_2^* > dY_2$ (24)

If $p_2(m_{13} m_{21} + m_{23} b_1) > (p_1 + p_2)(m_{12} m_{23} + m_{13} b_2)$, then $dY_3^* > dY_3$ (25)

If conditions (23)–(25) are satisfied, then all three countries have benefited from this trade-creating customs union.

Indicative Results

To explain these conditions I shall insert some hypothetical, but representative, values. These values and the range they cover are deliberately selected, so as to represent the realities of *actual* economies. There are two basic reasons for using hypothetical data. Firstly, the analysis adopted in this chapter does not attempt to find out whether or not trade creation has occurred, rather the *consequences* of trade creation when it actually takes place – this chapter is not about *empirical testing.* Secondly, as will shortly become evident, the actual values matter only in terms of the *extent* of gains and losses, but they do not matter when the *sign* of the changes is being considered, and this is the most significant factor in the analysis.

The data are given in table 7.1 and the results in table 7.2. The results suggest the following conclusions:

(i) Trade creation leads to an increase in national income in the partner country gaining the new employment and exports, but leads to a loss in income for the other partner country and for the outside world.

(ii) The gains and losses are a very small proportion of the amount of trade creation: the highest gain recorded is less than one tenth of trade creation and the highest loss is about one fifth of trade creation.

(iii) The higher (lower) the price differential, the higher (lower) the amount of loss and the lower (higher) the amount of gain (Cases 2 and 3).

Table 7.1 *Selected Representative Data*

Variable	P_1	P_2	t_1	t_2	t_3	s_1	s_2	s_3	m_{12}	m_{13}	m_{21}	m_{23}	m_{31}	m_{32}
Case 1	1.1	1	0.2	0.2	0.2	0.2	0.2	0.2	0.05	0.05	0.05	0.05	0.05	0.05
	1.2	1	0.3	0.3	0.3	0.3	0.3	0.3	0.1	0.1	0.1	0.1	0.1	0.1
	1.5	1	0.2	0.3	0.2	0.2	0.3	0.2	0.05	0.05	0.1	0.05	0.05	0.05
			0.3	0.2	0.2	0.3	0.2	0.2	0.05	0.05	0.05	0.10	0.05	0.05
			0.2	0.2	0.3	0.2	0.2	0.3	0.05	0.05	0.0	0.00	0.05	0.05
									0.00	0.05	0.05	0.05	0.05	0.05
									0.00	0.05	0.05	0.05	0.05	0.00
	Cases 2–3		Cases 4–7			Cases 8–11			Cases 12–17					

Note: Case 1 is the basic case. All other cases have the same values as case 1 except for the variables specified. For each group, the case number is to be read from top to bottom.

Table 7.2 *Indicative Results*

Case	$dY_1^* - dY_1$	$dY_2^* - dY_2$	$dY_3^* - dY_3$
1	–0.12121	+0.03255	–0.01715
2	–0.12772	+0.03100	–0.01860
3	–0.14725	+0.02635	–0.02325
4	–0.10121	+0.02465	–0.01595
5	–0.11029	+0.03255	–0.01495
6	–0.12121	+0.02735	–0.01805
7	–0.11129	+0.02945	–0.01705
8	–0.21801	+0.07215	–0.02145
9	–0.16489	+0.03255	–0.02545
10	–0.12121	+0.05335	–0.01305
11	–0.16089	+0.04495	–0.01705
12	–0.20516	+0.02300	–0.05060
13	–0.13551	+0.03255	–0.01980
14	–0.14076	+0.03255	–0.01455
15	–0.08736	+0.03255	–0.01680
16	–0.12121	+0.04685	–0.01430
17	–0.10166	+0.04160	–0.01430

(iv) The higher (lower) the income tax rates, the lower (higher) the gains and losses (Case 4). Cases 5–7 can be interpreted in the same fashion.

(v) The higher (lower) the marginal propensities to save, the higher (lower) the gains and losses (Case 8). Cases 9–11 can be interpreted accordingly.

(vi) The higher (lower) the marginal propensities to import, the higher (lower) the losses and the lower (higher) the gain. (Cases 12–17).

Alternative Possibilities

1. Now consider the case where there is full employment in countries 2 and 3, but less than full employment in country 1. Trade creation will result in the same expressions as before for countries 1 and 3 – given by equations (17) and (19). As for country 2, the term qp_2 must be eliminated, because in a fully employed economy this output can be achieved either at the expense of domestic production, at the expense of exports to country 3, or at the expense of alternative exports

to country 1. If it is at the expense of alternative exports to country 1, expressions (20), (22) and

$$dY_2^* = \frac{m_{12}dY_1 + m_{32}dY_3^* + dI_2}{b_2} \tag{21''}$$

are the relevant ones. These can be given in a form equivalent to equations (14)–(16). Hence:

$$\begin{aligned} dY_1^* = \{&[dI_1 - q(p_1 + p_2)](b_2 b_3 - m_{23}m_{32}) \\ &+ dI_2(m_{21}b_3 + m_{23}m_{31}) \\ &+ dI_3(m_{23}m_{32} + m_{31}b_2)\}/D \end{aligned} \tag{26}$$

$$\begin{aligned} dY_2^* = \{&[dI_1 - q(p_1 + p_2)](m_{13}m_{32} + m_{12}b_3) \\ &+ dI_2(b_1 b_3 - m_{13}m_{31}) \\ &+ dI_3(m_{23}m_{31} + m_{32}b_1)\}/D \end{aligned} \tag{27}$$

$$\begin{aligned} dY_3^* = \{&[dI_1 - q(p_1 + p_2)](m_{12}m_{23} + m_{13}b_2) \\ &+ dI_2(m_{13}m_{21} + m_{23}b_1) \\ &+ dI_3(b_1 b_2 - m_{12}m_{21})\}/D \end{aligned} \tag{28}$$

Comparing equations (26)–(28) with equations (14)–(16), it is quite evident that

$$dY_1 > dY_1^* \text{ by } \frac{q(p_1 + p_2)(b_2 b_3 - m_{23}m_{32})}{D} \tag{29}$$

$$dY_2 > dY_2^* \text{ by } \frac{q(p_1 + p_2)(m_{13}m_{32} + m_{12}b_3)}{D} \tag{30}$$

$$dY_3 > dY_3^* \text{ by } \frac{q(p_1 + p_2)(m_{12}m_{23} + m_{13}b_2)}{D} \tag{31}$$

Therefore, all three countries are worse off as a result of trade creation.

If the extra output is at the expense of exports to country 3, the relevant income expressions are those given by (26), (28) and:

$$dY_3^* = \frac{m_{13}dY_1^* + m_{23}dY_2^* + dI_3 + qp_2}{D} \tag{27'}$$

i.e. the decline in country 3's imports results in an increase in the real value of its income (which does not contradict the assumption of full employment) without the multiplier effect. Hence the result in this case is the same as that given by equations (20)–(22), but countries 2 and 3 are reversed and the effects are dampened because of the lack of repercussions in country 3.

If the extra output is at the expense of domestic production, then the relevant expressions are given by equations (20), (21″) and (22). Hence all three countries are worse off as a result of trade creation.

2. Now, consider the case where the newly made redundant resources in country 1 are to be absorbed elsewhere within the economy, so that there is full employment globally. There is of course no reason why such utilisation of resources should increase inefficiency in country 1: the reallocation is simply due to the discriminatory tariff removal. Those made redundant (by compulsion) would settle for equal pay elsewhere. If they had to accept lower pay, then one could argue that that would be due to their lower productivity rate in the new employment.

In such circumstances, one should add qp_1 to equation (17) and retain equations (19) and (21″) as expressions of the effect of trade creation. Hence, the income change expressions become equations (19), (21″) and:

$$dY_1^* = \frac{m_{21}dY_2^* + m_{31}dY_3^* + dI_1 - qp_2}{b_1} \tag{32}$$

Equations (19), (21″) and (22) can be expressed in a form equivalent to equations (14)–(16). Hence:

$$\begin{aligned} dY_1^* = \{ & (dI_1 - qp_2)(b_2b_3 - m_{23}m_{32}) \\ & + dI_2(m_{21}b_3 + m_{23}m_{31}) \\ & + dI_3(m_{21}m_{32} + m_{31}b_2)\}/D \end{aligned} \tag{33}$$

$$\begin{aligned} dY_2^* = \{ & (dI_1 - qp_2)(m_{13}m_{32} + m_{12}b_3) \\ & + dI_2(b_1b_3 - m_{13}m_{31}) \\ & + dI_3(m_{12}m_{31} + m_{32}b_1)\}/D \end{aligned} \tag{34}$$

$$dY_3^* = \{(dI_1 - qp_2)(m_{12}m_{23} + m_{13}b_2) + dI_2(m_{13}m_{21} + m_{23}b_1) + dI_3(b_1b_2 - m_{12}m_{21})\} / D \quad (35)$$

A comparison of equations (33)–(35) with equations (14)–(16) reveals that:

$$dY_1 > dY_1^* \text{ by } \frac{qp_2(b_2b_3 - m_{23}m_{32})}{D} \quad (36)$$

$$dY_2 > dY_2^* \text{ by } \frac{qp_2(m_{13}m_{32} + m_{12}b_3)}{D} \quad (37)$$

$$dY_3 > dY_3^* \text{ by } \frac{qp_2(m_{12}m_{23} + m_{13}b_2)}{D} \quad (38)$$

Hence all three countries are worse off as a result of trade creation, but the extent of the loss in this case is smaller than in the previous cases.

Conclusion

The conclusion of this section is that, given certain circumstances, trade creation discussed in a macro model is detrimental for both the customs union partner which loses domestic employment and for the outside world. It is beneficial for the partner which gains new employment and exports. However, the gains and losses represent a very significant proportion of the amount of trade creation.

Assuming full employment all round, trade creation is detrimental for all three countries of the world. The same conclusion holds true for intermediate cases.

It must be emphasised that this conclusion is not to be confused with either the standard conclusion, or with Yu and Scully's (1976, p. 12). This is because the model adopted here is different from theirs.

Trade Diversion

Starting from the initial situation as given by equations

(14)–(16), one is now interested in what happens to these 'normal' relationships as a result of the formation of a purely trade-diverting customs union.

Trade diversion occurs when cheap initial imports from the outside world are replaced by expensive imports from the customs union partner.[8] I shall assume that these diverted imports will be sold at a price equal to the import price plus the customs duty. Hence the customs union formation, apart from leading to the removal of mutual tariffs between countries 1 and 2, will also result in a certain amount of imports (q) that previously came into country 2 from country 3 being replaced by an equal amount from country 1.

These changes lead to:[9]

$$dY_1^* = \frac{m_{21}dY_2^* + m_{31}dY_3^* + dI_1 - qt_1^*}{b_1} \tag{39}$$

$$dY_2^* = \frac{m_{12}dY_1^* + m_{32}dY_3^* + dI_2 + q(1 + t_1^*)}{b_2} \tag{40}$$

$$dY_3^* = \frac{m_{13}dY_1^* + m_{23}dY_2^* + dI_3 - q}{b_3} \tag{41}$$

where the stars on the income changes indicate that these are the income changes resulting from the introduced disturbance.

I shall express these in the much tidier form of equations (14)–(16):

$$\begin{aligned} dY_1^* = \{&(dI_1 - qt_1^*)(b_2b_3 - m_{23}m_{32}) \\ &+ [dI_2 + q(1 + t_1^*)](m_{21}b_3 + m_{23}m_{31}) \\ &+ (dI_3 - q)(m_{21}m_{22} + m_{31}b_2)\} / D \end{aligned} \tag{42}$$

$$\begin{aligned} dY_2^* = \{&(dI_1 - qt_1^*)(m_{13}m_{32} + m_{12}b_3) \\ &+ [dI_2 + q(1 + t_1^*)](b_1b_3 - m_{13}m_{31}) \\ &+ (dI_3 - q)(m_{12}m_{31} + m_{32}b_1)\} / D \end{aligned} \tag{43}$$

$$\begin{aligned} dY_3^* = \{&(dI_1 - qt_1^*)(m_{12}m_{23} + m_{13}b_2) \\ &+ [dI_2 + q(1 + t_1^*)](m_{13}m_{21} + m_{23}b_1) \\ &+ (dI_3 - q)(b_1b_2 - m_{12}m_{21})\} / D \end{aligned} \tag{44}$$

Comparing equations (42)–(44) with equations (14)–(16),

one can specify the relationship between dY and dY^* for each country. If:

$$q(1 + t_1^*)(m_{21}b_3 + m_{23}m_{31}) > qt_1^*(b_2b_3 - m_{23}m_{32}) + q(m_{21}m_{32} + m_{31}b_2) \text{ then } dY_1^* > dY.$$

q can be dropped from both sides, hence if:

$$(1 + t_1^*)(m_{21}b_3 + m_{23}m_{31}) > t_1^*(b_2b_3 - m_{23}m_{32}) + (m_{21}m_{32} + m_{31}b_2) \quad (45)$$

then $dY_1^* > dY_1$

Similarly, if:

$$(1 + t_1^*)(b_1b_3 - m_{13}m_{31}) > t_1^*(m_{13}m_{32} + m_{12}b_3) + (m_{12}m_{31} + m_{32}b_1) \quad (46)$$

then $dY_2^* > dY_2$

And, if:

$$(1 + t_1^*)(m_{13}m_{21} + m_{23}b_1) > t_1^*(m_{12}m_{23} + m_{13}b_2) + (b_1b_2 - m_{12}m_{21}) \quad (47)$$

then $dY_3^* > dY_3$

Indicative Results

As before, it would be helpful to have some practical notions about these conditions. To make deductions from them, I shall again insert some hypothetical but representative values. The data are given in table 7.1 replacing the columns headed P_1 and P_2 with a column headed t_1^* with values: 0.2; 0.1; and 0.5. The results are given in table 7.3.

The results suggest the following:

(i) Trade diversion leads to a loss in income for country 1 and the rest of the world and results in a net gain for country 2. These gains and losses represent a very small fraction of the diverted trade – the highest figure is a gain of about 16%.

Table 7.3 *Indicative Results*

Case	$dY_1^* - dY_1$	$dY_2^* - dY_2$	$dY_3^* - dY_3$
1	–0.00992	+0.05952	–0.0496
2	–0.00496	+0.05456	–0.0496
3	–0.0248	+0.0744	–0.0496
4	–0.00812	+0.04872	–0.0406
5	–0.00788	+0.05952	–0.0442
6	–0.00992	+0.05428	–0.0456
7	–0.01008	+0.05348	–0.0496
8	–0.01872	+0.11232	–0.0936
9	–0.01808	+0.05952	–0.0712
10	–0.00992	+0.08048	–0.0656
11	–0.00928	+0.08368	–0.0496
12	–0.01472	+0.08832	–0.0736
13	–0.00192	+0.05952	–0.05760
14	–0.01152	+0.05952	–0.04800
15	–0.01632	+0.05952	–0.0432
16	–0.00992	+0.05152	–0.04160
17	–0.00832	+0.04992	–0.04160

(ii) Cases 2 and 3 in comparison with case 1 indicate that the higher (lower) country 1's tariff rate, the higher (lower) the amount of both gains and losses for all three countries.

(iii) Case 4 (in comparison with case 1) indicates that the higher (lower) the marginal tax rates, the lower (higher) the amounts of loss and gain. Cases 5–7 can be interpreted accordingly.

(iv) Case 8 (in comparison with case 1) suggests that the higher (lower) the marginal propensity to save, the higher (lower) the amount of gain and loss. Cases 9–11 can be interpreted in the same fashion.

(v) Case 12 (in comparison with case 1) shows that the higher (lower) the marginal propensities to import, the higher (lower) the amount of gains and losses. Cases 13–17 indicate similar results which should be interpreted with respect to the country experiencing a change in its marginal propensity to import.

Full Employment

Assuming full employment in all three countries, the gains and losses for countries 2 and 3 respectively cancel each other out because of a reallocation of resources. Hence the only loss is the tariff revenue to country 1. This depresses imports from countries 2 and 3 and therefore produces losses all round.

Conclusion

The conclusion of this section is that trade diversion is beneficial to the customs union partner gaining the new exports and is detrimental to the other partner and the outside world. However, the extent of the gains and losses is equal to an insignificant proportion of the diverted trade. This is due to the fact that the loss of exports by the outside world affects its imports from the partners through the marginal propensity to import and that the gain in exports by the partner concerned affects the latter's imports from the other two countries. These opposing forces soften the initial impact of trade diversion.

This conclusion should not be confused with that of a welfare-improving, trade-diverting customs union, simply because the analysis is conducted under macro conditions, with foreign repercussions and constant prices and coefficients.

Overall Conclusion

The advantage of a macroeconomic approach is that it clearly shows the once-and-for-all nature of trade creation and trade diversion.[10] Moreover, it also clearly demonstrates the insignificance of their impact given realistic values of the relevant coefficients. Finally, this approach clearly demonstrates that tariffs are a purely micro phenomenon.

Notes

1 Trade creation and trade diversion are discussed in specific detail in Chapters 2–5.

2 The discussion in this chapter is confined to customs unions only. Those readers interested in the differences between customs unions and free trade areas should consult Chapter 3.

3 Brown (1961) is the only exception. However, his analysis takes into account neither the differences between the situations prior to and after the customs union formation, nor the repercussions on the outside world.

4 El-Agraa (1978).

5 I am ignoring autonomous consumption and lagged relationships. Such refinements complicate the analysis without substantially altering the conclusions.

6 The proper import function is of course: $M = M(Y, \frac{P_d}{P_f}, \alpha)$, where f and d stand for foreign and domestic respectively and α is the rate of exchange; that is if one were to ignore the input-output function suggested by C.P. Kennedy and A.P. Thirlwall. Since prices (P), including the rate of exchange, are assumed to remain constant, this function is reduced to the simple form adopted in the analysis. It will become apparent later that any sophistication would not substantially alter the conclusions.

7 The derivation of these equations is straightforward if the reader is able to handle matrix algebra.

8 I am deliberately adopting Johnson's 1974 definition of trade diversion, so as to avoid the non-problem of a trade-diverting, welfare-improving customs union as formulated by Gehrels (1956/7) and Lipsey (1960) and revived by Bhagwati (1971) – see Chapter 2.

9 These equations are derived in the same fashion as the equivalent equations for trade creation.

10 This point is discussed in great detail in El-Agraa (1980), Chapter 5.

8

Is There an Economic Rationale for Customs Unions?

A M EL-AGRAA

The theory of international economic integration has failed to provide an *orthodox* rationale for customs union formation – see Chapters 2–5. This state of affairs can be attributed to several factors: unilateral non-discriminatory tariff reductions are always superior to customs unions (Cooper and Massell 1965a); the possible gains from favourable changes in terms of trade depend entirely on lack of retaliation by the outside world (Petith 1977); scale economies are difficult to achieve particularly in highly advanced economies where the scope for them is limited (Johnson 1958).

Since the gains from static resource reallocation, favourable changes in the terms of trade and scale economies between them exhaust the major areas of possible economic rationalisation of customs union formation, economists have had to resort to alternative explanations. These alternatives have come from Johnson (1965), who uses a political economy approach, and from Cooper–Massell (1965b), who demonstrate that two countries can together do more than each in isolation. These contributions have been criticised: '. . . the danger is that their argument lends itself easily to abuse by governments as a justification for whatever they have chosen or choose to do.' (Krauss 1972)

These matters have been discussed in great detail in Chapters 2 and 4. The purpose of this chapter is to utilise the macro model of the previous chapter to examine the Cooper–Massell policy of a unilateral tariff reduction being superior to customs union formation.

The Macro Approach

In Chapter 7 I discussed the implications of trade creation and trade diversion when considered under different yet orthodox assumptions. In this section I shall extend the conclusions reached there in order to deal with the topic of this chapter and then discuss the implications for an economic rationalisation of customs union formation.

Equations (14)–(16) of Chapter 7 are the starting point:

$$dY_1 = \{ dI_1 (b_2 b_3 - m_{23} m_{32}) + dI_2 (m_{21} b_3 + m_{23} m_{31}) + dI_3 (m_{21} m_{32} + m_{31} b_2) \} / D \quad (14)$$

$$dY_2 = \{ dI_1 (m_{13} m_{32} + m_{12} b_3) + dI_2 (b_1 b_3 - m_{13} m_{31}) + dI_3 (m_{12} m_{31} + m_{32} b_1) \} / D \quad (15)$$

$$dY_3 = \{ dI_1 (m_{12} m_{23} + m_{13} b_2) + dI_2 (m_{13} m_{21} + m_{23} b_1) + dI_3 (b_1 b_2 - m_{12} m_{21}) \} / D \quad (16)$$

where:

$$b_1 = s_1 (1 - t_1) + m_{12} + m_{13};$$
$$b_2 = s_2 (1 - t_2) + m_{21} + m_{23};$$
$$b_3 = s_3 (1 - t_3) + m_{31} + m_{32};$$
$$D = b_1 b_2 b_3 - m_{23} m_{32} b_1 - m_{12} m_{21} b_3 - m_{12} m_{23} m_{31} - m_{13} m_{21} m_{32} - m_{13} m_{31} b_2$$

These equations give a meaningful expression of the state of interdependence between the three countries in the initial situation of non-discriminatory protection. They are expressions of the multiplier relationships with foreign repercussions.

These equations can, therefore, be used to study the effect an autonomous change in investment (which could be taken to represent a change in *any* autonomous element) in any of the three countries would have on any or all of them.

Trade Creation and Trade Diversion

The establishment of the customs union results in the removal of tariff barriers between countries 1 and 2. Trade creation means that a certain quantity of output (q) that is initially produced domestically in country 1 is now to be imported from country 2. The original value of this output is qp_1, where p_1 is the price in country 1. The new value of this output is qp_2, where p_2 is the price in country 2. Trade creation means that $qp_1 > qp_2$, i.e. $p_1 > p_2$.

Trade diversion occurs when cheaper initial imports from the outside world are replaced by expensive imports from the customs union partner.[1] I shall assume that these diverted imports will be sold at a price equal to the import price plus the customs duty. Hence the customs union formation, apart from leading to the removal of mutual tariffs between countries 1 and 2, will also result in a certain amount of imports (q) that previously came into country 2 from country 3 being replaced by an equal amount from country 1.

Trade creation results in the following expressions:

$$dY_1^* = \{[dI_1 - q(p_1 + p_2)](b_2 b_3 - m_{23}m_{32}) + (dI_2 + qp_2)(m_{21}b_3 + m_{23}m_{31}) + dI_3(m_{21}m_{32} + m_{31}b_2)\} / D \quad (17)$$

$$dY_2^* = \{[dI_1 - q(p_1 + p_2)](m_{13}m_{32} + m_{12}b_3) + (dI_2 + qp_2)(b_1 b_3 - m_{13}m_{31}) + dI_3(m_{12}m_{31} + m_{32}b_1)\} / D \quad (18)$$

$$dY_3^* = \{[dI_1 - q(p_1 + p_2)](m_{12}m_{23} + m_{13}b_2) + (dI_2 + qp_2)(m_{13}m_{21} + m_{23}b_1) + dI_3(b_1 b_2 - m_{12}m_{21})\} / D \quad (19)$$

Trade diversion leads to the following expressions:

$$\begin{aligned} dY_1^* = \{&(dI_1 - qt_1^*)(b_2 b_3 - m_{23} m_{32}) \\ &+ [dI_2 + q(1 + t_1^*)]\,(m_{21} b_3 + m_{23} m_{31}) \\ &+ (dI_3 - q)(m_{21} m_{32} + m_{31} b_2)\} / D \end{aligned} \tag{20}$$

$$\begin{aligned} dY_2^* = \{&(dI_1 - qt_1^*)(m_{13} m_{32} + m_{12} b_3) \\ &+ [dI_2 + q(1 + t_1^*)]\,(m_{13} m_{21} + m_{23} b_1) \\ &+ (dI_3 - q)(m_{12} m_{31} + m_{32} b_1)\} / D \end{aligned} \tag{21}$$

$$\begin{aligned} dY_3^* = \{&(dI_1 - qt_1^*)(m_{12} m_{23} + m_{13} b_2) \\ &+ [dI_2 + q(1 + t_1^*)]\,(m_{13} m_{21} + m_{23} b_1) \\ &+ (dI_3 - q)(b_1 b_2 - m_{12} m_{21})\} / D \end{aligned} \tag{22}$$

A unilateral tariff reduction results in the income changes given by equations (14)–(16). This is because in this model tariffs do not affect the quantity of imports – the price elasticity of demand for imports is zero. This assumption is essential for excluding quantity changes from changes in the source of supply of imports. Otherwise, one is thrown back into the non-problem of trade-diverting/creating, welfare-improving/reducing customs unions which has been the main source of confusion in this area.

These expressions are too complicated to handle. In my papers and in Chapter 7, I used hypothetical, but representative, data in order to get some idea about the sign of the relevant changes. The data are those given in Chapter 7 and the results are those given in tables 7.2 and 7.3.

It is important to note the following conclusions:

(i) trade creation when compared with a unilateral tariff reduction is harmful to the partner losing output and employment (country 1), but is beneficial to the other partner;

(ii) trade diversion, when compared with a policy of unilateral tariff reduction, is harmful to the partner experiencing a change in its source of supply of imports (country 1), but it is beneficial to the partner gaining the new output and exports (country 2);

(iii) both trade creation and trade diversion are harmful to the outside world (country 3) in comparison with a policy of unilateral tariff reduction.

A Comparison

The Cooper–Massell approach clearly demonstrates that trade creation is beneficial while trade diversion is harmful and that the latter can be avoided by adopting a policy of unilateral tariff reduction. Johnson's approach suggests that trade diversion is good and trade creation may be good or bad. The two approaches lead more or less to opposite conclusions; in Johnson's case both trade creation and trade diversion may be economically more beneficial.

The macro approach indicates that both trade creation and trade diversion are bad for country 1 and the outside world, but beneficial for country 2. However, in a customs union one would expect trade creation and trade diversion to be spread between the two partners rather than concentrated on one partner only. When this dispersion effect is taken into account, then country 1 will be the loser in one case and the gainer in another, and vice versa for country 2. Hence it is certain that at least one partner will end up better off as a result of the customs union formation. The outside world is of course always a net loser.

To demonstrate that this result is not purely hypothetical, consider a case where country 1 replaces its own expensive domestic production (qp_1) by imports from country 2 (qp_2) and, at the same time, country 2 replaces initial imports from country 3 by imports from country 1. This amounts to country 1 experiencing trade creation and country 2 experiencing trade diversion. The resulting income changes are:

$$\begin{aligned} dY_1^* = {} & c_1 dY_1^*(1 - t_1) + dI_1 + m_{21} dY_2^* \\ & + m_{31} dY_3^* + q(1 + t_2^*) + t_1 dY_1^* \\ & + t_1^* dY_1^* m_{13} - qp_1 - dY_1^* m_{13}(1 + t_1^*) \\ & - dY_1^* m_{12} - qp_2 \end{aligned} \tag{23}$$

$$\begin{aligned} dY_2^* = {} & c_2 dY_2^*(1 - t_2) + dI_2 + m_{12} dY_1^* \\ & + m_{32} dY_3^* + qp_2 + t_2 dY_2^* + t_2^* dY_2^* m_{23} \\ & - t_2^* q - dY_2^* m_{23}(1 + t_2^*) + q(1 + t_2^*) \\ & - dY_2^* m_{21} - q(1 + t_2^*) \end{aligned} \tag{24}$$

$$\begin{aligned} dY_3^* = {} & c_3 dY_3^*(1 - t_3) + dI_3 + m_{13} dY_1^* \\ & + m_{23} dY_2^* - q + t_3 dY_3^* + t_3^* dY_3^*(m_{31} + m_{32}) \\ & - dY_3^*(m_{31} + m_{32})(1 + t_3^*) \end{aligned} \tag{25}$$

Simplifying and rearranging gives:

$$dY_1^* = \frac{m_{21} dY_2^* + m_{31} dY_3^* + dI_1 + q(1 + t_2^* - p_1 - p_2)}{b_1} \tag{26}$$

$$dY_2^* = \frac{m_{12} dY_1^* + m_{32} dY_3^* + dI_2 + q(p_2 - t_2^*)}{b_2} \tag{27}$$

$$dY_3^* = \frac{m_{13} dY_1^* + m_{23} dY_2^* + dI_3 - q}{b_3} \tag{28}$$

Expressing each equation in terms of its own income change gives:

$$\begin{aligned} dY_1^* = {} & \{[dI_1 + q(1 + t_2^* - p_1 - p_2)](b_2 b_3 - m_{23} m_{32}) \\ & + [dI_2 + q(p_2 - t_2^*)](m_{21} b_3 + m_{23} m_{31}) \\ & + (dI_3 - q)(m_{21} m_{32} + m_{31} b_2)\} / D \end{aligned} \tag{29}$$

$$\begin{aligned} dY_2^* = {} & \{[dI_1 + q(1 + t_2^* - p_1 - p_2)](m_{13} m_{32} + m_{12} b_3) \\ & + [dI_2 + q(p_2 - t_2^*)](b_1 b_3 - m_{13} m_{31}) \\ & + (dI_3 - q)(m_{23} m_{31} + m_{32} b_1)\} / D \end{aligned} \tag{30}$$

$$\begin{aligned} dY_3^* = {} & \{[dI_1 + q(1 + t_2^* - p_1 - p_2)](m_{12} m_{23} + m_{13} b_2) \\ & + [dI_2 + q(p_2 - t_2^*)](m_{13} m_{21} + m_{23} b_1) \\ & + (dI_3 - q)(b_1 b_2 - m_{12} m_{21})\} / D \end{aligned} \tag{31}$$

Comparing equations (29)–(31) with the initial equations (14)–(16), it is evident that whether or not the initial income changes exceed or fall short of the new income, changes will depend on whether or not:

$$(1 + t_2^* - p_1 - p_2)(b_2 b_3 - m_{23} m_{32}) + (p_2 - t_2^*)(m_{21} b_3 + m_{23} m_{31}) - (m_{21} m_{32} + m_{31} b_2) \gtrless 0 \text{ for } dY_1 \quad (32)$$

$$(1 + t_2^* - p_1 - p_2)(m_{13} m_{32} + m_{12} b_3) + (p_2 - t_2^*)(b_1 b_3 - m_{13} m_{31}) - (m_{23} m_{31} + m_{32} b_1) \gtrless 0 \text{ for } dY_2 \quad (33)$$

$$(1 + t_2^* - p_1 - p_2)(m_{12} m_{23} + m_{13} b_2) + (p_2 - t_2^*)(m_{13} m_{21} + m_{23} b_1) - (b_1 b_2 - m_{12} m_{21}) \gtrless 0 \text{ for } dY_3 \quad (34)$$

Using the data for case 1 given in table 8.1 and assuming that t_2^* is equal to 20% gives the results shown in table 8.1.

Table 8.1 *Indicative Results for Trade Creation, Trade Diversion and Unilateral Tariff Reduction*

Case	$dY_1^* - dY_1$	$dY_2^* - dY_2$	$dY_3^* - dY_3$
1	–0.06169	+0.02263	–0.06665
2	–0.07316	+0.02604	–0.06820
3	–0.07285	+0.00155	–0.07285
4	–0.05249	+0.01653	–0.05655
5	–0.05601	+0.02263	–0.06055
6	–0.06169	+0.01947	–0.06225
7	–0.05781	+0.01937	–0.06665
8	–0.10569	+0.05343	–0.11505
9	–0.08441	+0.02263	–0.09105
10	–0.06169	+0.03527	–0.08425
11	–0.07721	+0.03567	–0.06665
12	–0.11684	+0.00828	–0.12420
13	–0.06799	+0.02263	–0.07740
14	–0.07164	+0.02013	–0.07375
15	–0.04544	+0.02513	–0.04880
16	–0.06169	+0.02643	–0.05590
17	–0.05174	+0.03078	–0.05590

That is, there is a clear but insignificant gain for country 2, a clear yet insignificant loss for country 1 and a clear but not so insignificant loss for the outside world as a result of the customs union formation. However, a unilateral tariff reduction, in comparison with the initial situation of no customs union, gives zero results since both situations are depicted by equations (14)–(16). If it is legitimate to combine the effects of the customs union formation on countries 1 and 2, then a comparison of the customs union situation with unilateral tariff reduction shows that the former is inferior *all round* since the sum of the second and third columns for *all* cases gives negative values – i.e., both the partners (combined) and the outside world are *worse* off in a customs union situation.

As demonstrated in Chapter 7, these conclusions remain equally valid in conditions of full employment.

Conclusions

The conclusions of this chapter are:

(a) Cooper–Massell's criticism is valid in that, whether or not trade diversion and trade creation are good or bad, there is still no economic justification for the formation of customs unions;

(b) there is no inherent contradiction for the theory of customs unions in terms of the micro/macro dichotomy;

(c) the macro analysis clearly demonstrates the micro nature of tariffs – tariffs are, strictly speaking, a micro phenomenon.

Note

1 I am deliberately adopting Johnson's 1974 definition of trade diversion, so as to avoid the non-problem of a trade-diverting, welfare-improving customs union as formulated by Gehrels (1956/7) and Lipsey (1960) and revived by Bhagwati (1971) – see Chapter 2.

Bibliography

Arndt, S.W., On discriminatory *versus* non-preferential tariff policies, *The Economic Journal*, vol. 78, 1968. Also reprinted in Robson 1971.

Arndt, S.W., Customs unions and the theory of tariffs, *American Economic Review*, vol. LIX, 1969.

Arrow, K., Chenery, H.B., Minhas, B.S. and Solow, R.M., Capital–labour substitution and economic efficiency, *Review of Economics and Statistics*, vol. XLIII, 1961.

Arrow, K. and Hahn, F.H., *General Competitive Analysis*, Oliver & Boyd 1971.

Balassa, B., *The Theory of Economic Integration*, Allen and Unwin, 1961.

Balassa, B., Trade creation and trade diversion in the European Common Market, *The Economic Journal*, vol. 77, 1967. Also reprinted in Robson 1971.

Balassa, B., Types of economic integration, in Machlup 1976.

Batra, R.N., *Studies in the Pure Theory of International Trade*, Macmillan 1975.

Bhagwati, J., Customs unions and welfare improvement, *The Economic Journal, vol. 81, 1971.*

Brown, A.J., Economic separatism *versus* a common market in developing countries, *Bulletin of Economic Research*, vol. 13, 1961.

Brown, A.J., Common market criteria and experience, *Three Banks Review*, vol. 57, 1963.

Burns, M.E., A note on the concept and measure of consumer's surplus, *American Economic Review*, vol. 63, 1973.

Burrows, B., Denton, G.R. and Edwards, G., *Federal Solutions to European Issues*, Macmillan Press 1977.

Collier, P., The welfare effects of customs union: an anatomy, *The Economic Journal,* vol. 89, 1979.

Cooper, C.A. and Massell, B.F., A new look at customs union theory, *The Economic Journal*, vol. 75, 1965a. Also reprinted in Robson 1971.

Cooper, C.A. and Massell, B.F., Towards a general theory of customs unions in developing countries, *Journal of Political Economy*, vol. 73, 1965b.

Corden, W.M., *Recent Developments in the Theory of International Trade,* Princeton University, International Finance Section, 1965.

Corden, W.M., Economies of scale and customs union theory, *Journal of Political Economy*, vol. 80, 1972.

Corden, W.M., *Trade Policy and Economic Welfare,* Oxford University Press 1974.

Curzon, V., *The Essentials of Economic Integration,* Macmillan for the Trade Policy Research Centre 1974.

Denton, G.R. (ed.), *Economic Integration in Europe,* Weidenfeld and Nicolson 1969.

Dutta, A., Domestic market distortions and customs unions: a geometrical analysis, *Journal of Development Studies,* vol. 5, No. 2, 1969.

El-Agraa, A.M., On deflation of production and investment in free trade areas, *Leeds Discussion Papers*, No. 62, 1978a.

El-Agraa, A.M., Customs unions *versus* free trade areas, *Leeds Discussion Papers,* No. 63, 1978b.

El-Agraa, A.M., On trade diversion, *Leeds Discussion Papers,* No. 66, 1978c.

El-Agraa, A.M., On trade creation, *Leeds Discussion Papers,* No. 67, 1978d.

El-Agraa, A.M., On optimum tariffs, retaliation and international co-operation, *Bulletin of Economic Research,* May 1979a.

El-Agraa, A.M., On tariff bargaining, *Bulletin of Economic Research,* August, 1979b.

El-Agraa, A.M., Common markets in developing countries, in *Inflation, Development and Integration: Essays in Honour of A.J. Brown,* Leeds University Press 1979c.

El-Agraa, A.M., *The Economics of the European Community,* Philip Allan 1980.

EFTA, *Convention Establishing the European Free Trade Association,* Geneva, 1960.

EFTA, *Structure, Rules and Operation,* Geneva, 1976.

Floystad, G., Trade-diverting customs unions, welfare and factor market imperfections, *Weltwirt.Archiv*, vol. 111, 1975.

Gehrels, F., Customs unions from a single country viewpoint, *Review of Economic Studies,* vol. 24, 1956–57.

Graaf, J de V., On optimal tariff structures, *Review of Economic Studies,* vol. 27, 1949–50.

Haldi, J., Economies of scale in industrial plants, *Journal of Political Economy*, vol. 75, 1972.

Hazelwood, A., The 'shiftability' of industry and the measurement of gains and losses in the East African Common Market, *Bulletin of the Oxford University Institute of Economics and Statistics*, vol. 26, 1966.

Hazelwood, A., *African Integration and Disintegration*, Oxford University Press 1967.

Hazelwood, A., *Economic Integration: The East African Experience*, Heinemann 1975.

Hazelwood, A., The East African Common Market: importance and effects, *Bulletin of the Oxford University Institute of Economics and Statistics*, vol. 28, 1976.

Hicks, J.R., *Value and Capital*, Oxford University Press, 1939.

Hodges, M. (ed.), *European Integration*, Penguin 1972.

Humphrey, D.D. and Ferguson, C.E., The domestic and world benefits of a customs union, *Economia Internazionale*, vol. 13, 1960.

Johnson, H.G., The criteria of economic advantage, *Bulletin of the Oxford University Institute of Economics and Statistics*, vol. 19, 1957.

Johnson, H.G., The gains from freer trade with Europe: an estimate, *Manchester School*, vol. 73, 1958.

Johnson, H.G., *Money, Trade and Economic Growth*, Allen and Unwin 1962, Chapter 3.

Johnson, H.G., An economic theory of protectionism, tariff bargaining and the formation of customs unions, *Journal of Political Economy*, vol. 73, 1965a. Also reprinted in Robson 1971.

Johnson, H.G., Optimal trade intervention in the presence of domestic distortions, in Baldwin *et al.*, *Trade Growth and the Balance of Payments*, Rand McNally 1965b.

Johnson, H.G., Trade-diverting customs unions: a comment, *The Economic Journal*, vol. 81, 1974.

Johnson, H.G. and Krauss, M.B., *General Equilibrium Analysis*, Allen and Unwin 1974.

Jones, A.J., The theory of economic integration, in *Inflation, Development and Integration: Essays in Honour of A.J. Brown*, University of Leeds Press 1979.

Jones, A.J., Domestic distortions and customs union theory, *Bulletin of Economic Research*, May 1980.

Kahnert, F. *et al.*, *Economic Integration Among Developing Countries*, Development Centre of the OECD, Paris, 1969.

Kemp, M.C., *A Contribution to the General Equilibrium Theory of Preferential Trading*, North-Holland Publishing Co. 1969.

Kemp, M.C., and Wan, H.Y., An elementary proposition concerning the formation of customs unions, *Journal of International Economics*, vol. 6, 1976.

Krauss, M.B., Recent developments in customs union theory: an interpretative survey, *Journal of Economic Literature*, vol. 10, 1972.

Leontief, W.W., Composite commodities and the problem of index numbers, *Econometrica*, vol. 4, 1936.

Lipsey, R.G., The theory of customs unions: trade diversion and welfare, *Economica*, February 1957.

Lipsey, R.G., The theory of customs unions: a general survey, *The Economic Journal*, September 1960.

Lipsey, R.G. *The Theory of Customs Unions: A General Equilibrium Analysis*, Weidenfeld and Nicolson 1970.

Machlup, F. (ed.), *Economic Integration Worldwide, Regional Sectoral*, Macmillan Press 1976.

Machlup, F., *A History of Thought on Economic Integration*, Macmillan Press 1977.

Massell, B.F., A reply, and further thoughts on customs unions, *The Economic Journal*, vol. 78, 1968.

Massell, B.F., *East African Economic Union: An Evaluation and Some Implications for Policy*, The Rand Corporation, Santa Monica, 1973.

Mead, D.C., The distribution of gains in customs unions between developing countries, *Kyklos*, vol. 21, 1968. Reprinted in Robson 1971.

Meade J.E., *The Theory of Customs Unions*, North-Holland Publishing Co. 1955a.

Meade, J.E., *The Theory of International Economic Policy, Vol. II: Trade and Welfare*, Oxford University Press 1955b.

Melvin, J.R., Comments on the theory of customs unions, *Manchester School*, vol. 37, 1969.

Metwally, M.M., Market limitation and industrialisation in Arab countries, in Bowers, J.K. (ed.), *Inflation, Development and Integration: Essays in Honour of A.J. Brown*, Leeds University Press 1979.

Michaely, M., On customs unions and the gains from trade, *The Economic Journal*, vol. 75, 1965.

Michaely, M., The assumptions of Jacob Viner's theory of customs unions, *Journal of International Economics*, vol. 6, 1976.

Mikesell, R.F., The theory of common markets as applied to regional arrangements among developing countries, in Harrod, R. and Hague, D. (eds), *International Trade Theory in a Developing World*, 1960. Reprinted in Robson 1971.

Minhas, B.S., The homohypallagic production function, factor-intensity reversals, and the Heckscher–Ohlin theorem, *Journal of Political Economy*, vol. 73, 1965.

Negishi, T., Customs unions and the theory of second best, *International Economic Review*, vol. 10, 1969.

Newlyn, W.T., Gains and losses in the East African Common Market, *Bulletin of Economic Research*, vol. 17, 1965.

Newlyn, W.T., The 'shiftability' of industry and the measurement of gains and losses in the East African Common Market: a reply, *Bulletin of the Oxford University Institute of Economics and Statistics*, vol. 28, 1966.

Petith, H.C., European integration and the terms of trade, *The Economic Journal*, vol. 87, 1977.

Pinder, J., *Problems of European Integration,* in Denton, G.R. (ed.), 1969.

Raisman Report, Colonial Office, *East Africa: Report of the Economic and Fiscal Commission,* Cmnd. 1279, 1961.

Robson, P. and Due, J.F., Tax harmonisation in the East African Common Market, in Shoup, C.S. *Fiscal Harmonisation in Common Markets,* Columbia University Press, 1967, vol. II; and Lury, D.A. (ed.), *The Economies of Africa,* Allen & Unwin, 1969.

Robson, P., (ed.), *International Economic Integration,* Penguin 1971.

Scitovsky, T., *Economic Theory and Western European Integration,* Stamford 1958.

Scitovsky, T., International trade theory and economic integration as a means of overcoming the disadvantages of a small nation, in Robinson, E.A.G. (ed.), *Economic Consequences of the Size of the Nations,* Macmillan 1963.

Shibata, H., The theory of economic unions: a comparative analysis of customs unions, free trade areas, and tax unions, in Shoup, C.S., *Fiscal Harmonisation in Common Markets, Vol. I: Theory,* Columbia University Press 1967. Also reproduced, abridged, in Robson, P., *International Economic Integration,* Penguin Modern Economics Readings 1971.

Swan, D., *The Economics of the Common Market,* Penguin Modern Economics Texts 1978.

Takayama, A., *International Trade,* Holt Rinehart & Winston 1972.

Tinbergen, J., *International Economic Integration,* Elsevier 1954.

Vanek, J., *General Equilibrium of International Discrimination,* Harvard University Press 1965.

Viner, J., *The Customs Union Issue,* Carnegie Endowment for International Peace, New York, 1950.

Williamson, J.E., Taped discussion with Johnson, H.G. on Britain and the EEC, Audio-Learning Ltd, London, 1962.

Williamson, J.E., On estimating the income effect of British entry to the EEC, *Survey Papers in Economics,* Guildford, 1971.

Yu, E.S. and Scully, G.W., Domestic distortions and the theory of customs unions, *Southern Economic Journal,* vol. 42, 1976.

Index